Anything
is Possible

Anything is Possible

A SELECTION OF ELEVEN WOMEN POETS

EDITED BY
MARY DI MICHELE

MOSAIC PRESS
OAKVILLE NEW YORK LONDON

Canadian Cataloguing in Publication Data

Main entry under title:
Anything is possible : a selection of 11 women poets

ISBN 0-88962-252-3 (bound). - ISBN 0-88962-251-5 (pbk.)

1. Canadian poetry (English) - 20th century. *
2. Canadian poetry (English) - Women authors. *
I. Di Michele, Mary, 1949-

PS8283.W^A 59 1984   C811'.54'0809287   C84-098745-5
PR9195.3.A59 1984

Published by Mosaic Press, P.O. Box 1032, Oakville, Ontario, L6J 5E9, Canada.

Published with the assistance of the Canada Council and the Ontario Arts Council.

Design by Doug Frank
Typeset by Speed River Graphics
Printed and bound in Canada

ISBN 0-88962-252-3 cloth
ISBN 0-88962-251-5 paper

Distributed in the United States by Flatiron Books, 175 Fifth Avenue, Suite 814, New York, N.Y. 10010, U.S.A.

Distributed in the U.K. by John Calder (Publishers) Ltd., 18 Brewer Street, London, W1R 4AS, England.

Distributed in New Zealand and Australia by Pilgrims South Press, P.O. Box 5101, Dunedin, New Zealand.

CONTENTS

INTRODUCTION — SPRING 1983

If "this century will do away with the concept of greatness," as Roo Borson observes in "Prognostications, Highway 27" — if that concept has not indeed been "old hat" for some time, then where do we find the energy, the courage, the imagination, to transcend our lives, to change our history. Our models are jaded, discredited and we, as women, have had very few models to work from anyway. Is that an advantage at this point in time I wonder?

Anything is Possible is a collection of the work of 11 poets. Unlike most anthologies it attempts to represent the poets by making a significant selection from new work, enough to convey their particular voice and view. These are writers whose poetry I have been following closely for some time. Jan Conn and Rosemary Sullivan, who do not have books published yet (although Jan Conn has two forthcoming), I discovered while working as poetry editor for *Toronto Life*. Several are poets local to Toronto, whose work engaged me particularly at readings. Bronwen Wallace and I published a collection together with Oberon Press: *Bread and Chocolate/Marrying into the Family* in the fall of 1980 and she has made the selection of my work included here. This anthology cannot be representative of all poets writing in this country. It is only trying to be representative of the voices of the poets included. (There is a renaissance of fine writing in every region.) These poets in particular are exploring the limits of the notion of the perfectibility of people, honing, devising an acute and passionate language.

This collection represents a new generation of women writers whose language is a kind of truth serum, asking pointed question of the speaker as well as the words themselves spoken. With deep feeling, but without sentimentality, these poets describe the world as they see it. Because they are women to whom the world of feeling has been abandoned by many men and because they are incisively intelligent, their work has a special integrity and a facility to illuminate some vital areas of experience which have been ignored by our literature to date. It is no coincidence that some of the finest poetry in this country is being written by women. It is a question of what needs to be said and who is best equipped, at this historical point in time, to say it.

The politics of these poets has little to do with the process or machinations of an act of parliament (more the pity for parliament) but a lot to do with what we consciously choose to value, how we are *determined* to live. A discouraged Adrienne Rich writes: "This is how I would live if I could choose:/ this is what is possible." This anthology opens with Marilyn Bowering's poem: "Leavetaking," the first line of which is: "Language says: anything is possible" — from which I derived the title for this anthology. The collection ends with Bronwen Wallace's "A Simple Poem for Virginia Woolf," a poem which describes the kinds of restraints that women experience socially, which often, in fact, most often, circumscribe what is possible. We are too wise, too sophisticated to look for heroes among us, but the heroic is a vital energy or impulse; a kind of collective courage and generosity is needed to transform our world.

A Note About The Editor

Mary di Michele, born in 1949, is the author of four books: *Trees of August*, Three Trees Press, Toronto, 1978; *Bread and Chocolate*, Oberon Press, 1980; *Mimosa and Other Poems*, Mosaic Press, 1981, reprinted in 1983; and, forthcoming from Oberon Press: *Necessary Sugar*, in 1984. She is first prize winner for poetry in the CBC competition 1980. She has worked as poetry editor for *Toronto Life* and currently for *Poetry Toronto*. Her major projects now are an anthology of poetry on sexual politics with Pier Giorgio di Cicco and a manuscript of lyric poems: *Moon Sharks*.

ACKNOWLEDGEMENTS

I would like to thank: Marilyn Bowering and Press Porcépic for poems used from *Giving Back Diamonds*, 1982; "Learning the Bomb" was published in *Malahat Review*.

There are many things I would like to thank Roo Borson for, here for her contributions to this anthology, others it would take a summer of days to even begin to tell. Some of the poems included were published in *Toronto Life, Fireweed, Quarry, Ethos, Canadian Forum, Waves, Saturday Night*.

Thank you Jan Conn for your contributions to this anthology. Some of the poems included here have appeared in *Prism International* and *Room of One's Own*.

I wish to thank Lorna Crozier, formerly Lorna Uher, for her contributions to this anthology, as well as *Grain* and *Saturday Night* where some of these poems have appeared.

Thank you Susan Glickman for your contributions to this anthology, for your golden line and for the example of your physical and intellectual discipline. Some of the poems here have appeared in *Event, This Magazine, Canadian Forum, Quarry, Hanging Loose, Descant*, and *The Inner Ear* (Quadrant Editions) edited by Gary Geddes.

I would like to thank Erin Mouré for her contributions to and interest in this project as well as the House of Anansi for poems included here from her collection: *Wanted Alive*. Some of the work included here has previously been published in *Northern Light, Canadian Literature, Room of One's Own, Arc*. I would also like to thank Howie White of Harbour Publishing for letting us use "Tricks".

I would like to thank Libby Scheier for permission to use her work for this anthology. Some of these poems were published in *The Larger Life* (Black Moss Press), and magazines: *Toronto Life, Dalhousie Review, Descant, Prism International, Tamarack Review*.

I would like to thank Carolyn Smart not only for her contributions to this anthology, but for providing recent evidence that not only is anything possible, but the best that we can imagine may be. Some of her poems included here have appeared in the collections: *Swimmers in Oblivion* (York Publishing), *Power Sources* (Fiddlehead), as well as *Toronto Life* and *Malahat Review*.

I would like to thank Rosemary Sullivan for the energy and intelligence she brings to Canadian poetry as well as for her contributions to this anthology. Some of these poems have appeared in *Toronto Life, Descant, Montreal Review*.

How can I ever thank Bronwen Wallace enough, for her intelligence, her enlightenment, her courage? I'm in awe of this woman who has such adult assurance and knowledge, with a child's sense of play, of fun. Let me just thank you here for the poems you've contributed to this anthology, some of which have been published in *Canadian Forum*, *Event*, *Fireweed*, and *Signs of the Former Tenant* for which I would like to give special thanks to Oberon Press.

ANYTHING IS POSSIBLE

ROO BORSON

THE WHOLE NIGHT, COMING HOME

Low white garden fences, glossy leaves
of camelia and lemon after rain.
After dinner, walking, just for a breath
of air away from the family.
The Johnstons' yard glistens
though it's not theirs anymore.
Someone else lives there.   Still
they're Nick Johnston's lemon trees.

The firs, their shaggy branches full of rain.
The big rock where all the kids used to play,
building forts around it.   Now
it's haunted, more than empty.

Through the mist, the clearing rain,
the whole city blinks like a jet on a runway,
you can hear the engines rev, forever, going nowhere.

The bench that used to look out over it,
where we sat for hours, for those few years,
trying out kisses on first lovers: this time
it's gone.   Four marks in the ground.
And the eucalyptus trees
still fluttering over it, with stars between the leaves.

We could own anything then,
just by being there, when the owners were asleep.
We had the whole city, the whole night.
It's possible to come back
but none of it's yours anymore.   It belongs
to someone else.   But where are they?
Asleep like their parents?   Or have they found
new places, places you don't know how to find
because you don't need them enough anymore.

BLACKBERRIES

The eucalyptus shadows hang
like knives, knives that cut nothing,
shadows.   A breeze starts up
like a little thrill
going through a crowd.   The wet smoke smell.
A shadow shivers over the hills
and the two girls still picking blackberries
down in the bushes stop and listen.
They've been told about this wind.   They've been told
it can get you pregnant, that in the dark spaces
between bushes sometimes a man crouches.
That at the sight of a girl a man
just goes crazy, he can't help himself.
They keep picking, but faster.   All they want
is some blackberries.   Their mothers tell them that someday
they'll get more than they bargained for
staying out this late.   They know they should be going.
But the sun leaks out again, dimly,
then floods over the bushes, over their hands and faces,
a heat which turns their skin white again
and sparkles on the leaves.   The blackberries
are taut and warm and sweet; the kernels shine
like the thoraxes of solitary ants making their way
across the dirt.   The girls have a game
with sunlight, they pretend
it makes them invisible.   But around their mouths
and on their fingers the ragged pink stains
will take a long, long time to go away.

THE WAYS WE'RE TAUGHT

So he takes her to a place in the hills where he
thinks she'll give in to him.
That's what he's been taught:
girls can't resist pretty things.
So he shows her how the lights
shine through the trees
and then undoes his pants.
That's what they've been taught,
the girl to let herself be taken
so far and then say no, the boy
to try for anything.
The hills just lie there like rumpled velvet,
and the skull of the moon floats out of them.
This is what it is to be fifteen
and not know what to make of being alive.
The party was loud.   If you drink a little
the music takes care of everything,
it lifts you off the floor, dancing forward
at unknown miles an hour until somebody
falls down and has to be dragged outside.
It's easy to drink too much,
to let it all get away with you.
There's always somebody who never learns
what a bottle and a couple of pills can do.
Still, they've always woken up, telling the story
of how beautiful the tall cool trees look
when you're falling backwards.
So nobody's too shaken up,
somebody thinks to put on another record
and keep dancing.   Feelings,
they run so much smoother
when they're riding on the notes
of somebody else's song.
Its easier to feel anything
once it's been said before.
The girls, they're all looking around
for a boy who'll give them anything,
and the boys know it, they've been taught
to take what they can get.
So he offers her a ride home.
He says he'll show her something along the way.

SIXTEEN

All night she's lain listening to the rain
dropping like small change into puddles.
Trying to lie still beside the boy.

It's cold outside, grey and dripping from the eaves.
Each step seems to lift her
a foot off the ground from lack of sleep.
The houses — soaked through and strangely bright.
A cat prances up sideways
then scoots off through the bushes
deep in its own wildness.

The high school where they both go:
the fence pulled shut with a chain.
She can smell the hamburger places:
heat, grease, fresh donuts.
A smell vaguely like fog, vaguely like coffee.
The traffic lights go from gold to red to green
and back again.

The boy's bed was quiet, a damp heat under the blankets.
The room in the backyard over the garage,
his own world.   A drunken mother
asleep in the big house.

She only stayed because he told her to.   Or because
it's different from being alone.   But while he slept
she couldn't move.   As she walks
there's something she's not telling herself.
She's not allowing the words to form.

She's seen it.   Like two animals.
The tomcat bites the scruff
of the female's neck so she can't get away;
you can hear it hurting her and still she wants it.
The girl doesn't want it though.   It's not that
she wants.   She wants the part he keeps to himself,
what's back of those eyes.

ENDURANCE

You're sitting there drinking.
Big windows overlook the bay,
little chinks of light opening and closing
on the water, too quick to catch hold of.
It's one of the signs — a wallet stuffed full
with not just money but cards, things
with your name on them, an address.
One of the signs
that things are half over.
All around the room the sunset
glows in people's drinks; it lights up yours too.
Looking out at the bay
you can sit and smoke,
sort things out alone.
In the corner a woman's hair
shivers with chance sunlight as she laughs;
the man she's with — his eyes
keep flicking down to her sweater.
When people first meet
they smile a lot, testing.
But you have to meet first.
So things are half over, what of it?
Tiny rainbows on the walls
where the sun splits through the drinks.
On the bay the lights open and close,
too quick to catch.
It's like that, isn't it.
Everyone will go their way.   Eventually
you'll go yours too,
step again over the threshold
of a wrong house, a mistaken address.
The the meal eaten, hardly speaking.
Those kids — how could they ever have come from
nothing, from two bodies.   Now things are half over
and it's like it never happened.   And later
lying all night in the darkness
beside the real distance, a distance
like the long open ocean past San Francisco Bay
that you'd gladly dive in and swim except you know
it goes on forever, beyond
the endurance of the body.

IT'S NEVER ENOUGH

Something about the time of afternoon.
Sunlight singes the tall wisps of straw and somehow
nothing's worth doing except lying down and drowsing
in the warm dust, the mint and lemon smell
of eucalyptus.   Quick little winds shiver through
the trees and are gone; they hint
at a storm that doesn't come, ever.
And the little earth-tremors that say: someday.

Calico hills.   The huge circumference of shadow
around each tiny oak.
You can see perfectly, even at a distance,
the miniature of light and dark in the leaves,
you can see it
with your eyes closed.   The dull buzz
of motorcycles cutting up and down the hills.
The buzzing goes round and round
all sunny afternoons like this,
and the interminable construction of houses:
the saws, the hammers clunking away at dead wood.

All the sounds are hollow, and they carry forever.
It's the sound of a crazy person butting his head against a wall.
The sound of a woman tapping fingers to a music
she's making up in her head and isn't telling.

Those bikers.   I've seen first hand
how they smash into walls
and come out alive.   Finding out
how far they can push those machines,
how much abuse they can take.
They want to see
if their bodies are any different from that,
if a life
is different from that.   I know what they're after.

They'll push a woman into a corner where she can't
say no.   Even though she knows
exactly what they're doing to her, and knows
they do it just because
they're careless, deliberate.
She's learned to need that violence, that searching,
even if it's secondhand.   She needs to know
that the world could blow up at a footfall; there's that danger
that makes it all worth something.   And she needs them
to come back with that look in their eyes:

that insane sadness that can't be touched.
Something about the time of afternoon,
these bright, empty hills.
A biker shrieking around the short
hard curves like a penned-up goat
cracking his horns on the walls.

But all that is far away, a dull hollow buzz.   The sun
sinks low and shows through the poison oak: emeralds and blood.
Afternoon's a good time for drowsing,
but evening won't be: the damp darkness in which
if you had a lover you'd take his hand and say:
let's go somewhere warm.   But because you're alone
you'll have to remind yourself to get going.
So you close your eyes one more time to feel the sun
going down through the lids.   It won't last long.   It never does.

BALANCE

If you stand perfectly still and don't blink
you can see the horizon roll
against the rising moon.   The motion's
just a little bumpy; if you don't blink you can see it.

People like to look up and see the moon.
They don't even know why they like it.
Their eyes are just pulled.

Sometimes a pair of lovers kisses in the night grass.
And then the one on top, the man, catches it
nudging around a tree: the huge face
of everything he doesn't know,
a face full of blood.   But more than that:
the thing is so distant he knows
he'll never know it, never get anywhere close.
There's nothing like that face
to make him pull nearer to the girl, but also
it makes him want to look away.

What's a man to do with his own insides?
How can he reconcile
the girl and this moon,
how can he put a world together?

The girl is angry when he gets like this.
After all, she wants
what she wants.   All men are drifters.
They're like seeds of milkweed.
The slightest wind can push them
in the wrong direction and then they root there.

A woman, she has the hard job.
Once she finally has a family
she has to watch them all, even her husband.
She has to herd them here and there making sure
they stay together.   Any one of them could drift off.
Except the girls.   They can handle
more than a man.   Their feet are full of lead.
Somehow they know how to look at the moon
and still stay put.

Only once, the lovers were lying in the grass,
they were feeling loose that night, and she got on top.
But then in the middle of everything
she accidentally looked up.
And she saw it too.

FLYING LOW

On the hundred hills
the straw signals in the wind.
Sometimes a whole arc of it shines.

Every family is different, but in each one
they have the same eyes.
Every time they look at one another
there's that mirror.
There's no help for it.

Our family's eyes are the color of mud,
of cliffs, full
of tiny landslides that amount to nothing.
They are the sheen on puddles,
the sun that doesn't see anything better to light up.

Of my two brothers the elder is always watching
the younger, and the younger is always going somewhere.
Or he used to be;   right now
he's flying us in circles over the hills
where we all grew up.   That small cross of shadow
is us, twisting into a bird, a straight line.

Families are all the same.   They talk to one another
inside their heads, thinking the others can hear.

The sunset flashes on our faces as we twist away
over the shoreline, over the pale red foam,
but our tiny shadow stays back in the hills, rumpling over them,
over that spot we all know.   Long ago
each of us fell and hurt himself
one too many times and opened those eyes
that could have been any one of ours

to his own face reflected in the dirt.

SUMMER'S DRUG

Those nights.   They came after the days during which my
father's cigarette glowed like a rose caught in sunset on a
distant hillside. Then he would stub it out and night would fall.

The air would be traversed by strange scents emanating
from night-blooms, and the passion-vine broadcast for miles
around its coded message, wound along the trellis. The fruit
dangled, frosted with silver and fur, and inside: a smile of
translucent teeth, a mouth full of smuggled jewels. The
honeysuckle threaded everything with white and yellow
trumpets, evaporating in a sweet gas. So sweet that one
inhalation inflames the nostrils and after that is no longer
detected.

All night long my parents slept, breathing it, my mother
facing that darkened place she would always roll toward, the
open window to the wild hill. And my father next to her under
the light, fallen asleep in the middle of himself as in a field he'd
been crossing, the book still open beneath his fingers, and the
circling moths, with wings of powdered lead, whirling shadows
around his face.

THE NARCISSUS

At night the earth takes its place among the planets. The daffodils dim to the ghost of yellow, but their oniony smell seems to color the stars. Stars of scorched ice higher than cathedral windows. In the streets the dogs move like space-walkers over a dead planet, sniffing, remeasuring everything by smell, dispossessed. In daylight they'd wag their tails up and down the block without a thought. But dogs' ideas are close to the surface of their skulls: they sense the strangeness but can't act it out, except by sitting at attention in the dim street, their long black shadows sunk into it, the eye of a needle.

A pond on a spring night becomes a musical instrument. Now and then the plucking of the water, where something of its own volition startles, and a cascade of droplets picks out the notes. Just there the pond lies, rimmed with mud, but the narcissus droop their star-shaped heads at the ground, exiled by inches. Exiled and unmirrored.

BEAUTY

On these leaden days of early spring even one stray tentacle of shadowy sun makes the ground steam. There is a slate-green dust which frosts the backsides of certain trees, away from the wind, which three young girls have just discovered. They go from trunk to trunk finding the brighter shades, streaking it above their eyes, posing for one another. A few of last summer's blackberries are left hanging like lanterns in a storm of brambles, too deep for the birds and too high for things that crawl the ground at night. Still the half-fermented juice is good for staining the lips. The girls are just learning about beauty.

One day they'll be shown what their own beauty or lack of it will do to them. Not one day, but many nights, nights they'll lie alone sifting through incidents, certain instances which are the only analogue of those steeply lenthening bones, the breasts filling calmly, immutably as lakes taking in all that stormy and random rain.

ST. FRANCIS

For the last weeks the daylight hours have fallen short and
shorter. Transfixed by yellow porchlight to a wicked chartreuse,
shadow-plants spring up all around. Enamel primroses, and
snowdrops looking down like tiny streetlamps from their tall
stems. The garden bears its losses with a quiet we have never
accustomed ourselves to: even the crickets have taken their
gypsy music elsewhere.

    The little St. Francis looks out from his jagged pulpit
perched high on the cedar trunk, clay birds landing on his clay
shoulders. He'd be lost without them, for they were born that
way, joined. Like all saints he gazes straight ahead at a single
point. The black veils of the cedar boughs shade him; he is frail,
and they live here.

    As the youngest, I remember when my father and brothers
used to work outdoors. They'd go halfway around the house
just to douse the crooked ring of cedars under St. Francis with
their urine. Standing beside one another or alone they seemed
distanced, as if in some animistic prayer.

    But I remember St. Francis most for those April dawns
when I was the first awake. The amaryllis siphoned its pinkness
from underground springs of cologne. The sun would just
touch him and he'd blush as if a woman had come too near,
and all day the jays would land and take off again, taunting him
like delinquent boys, for he was no bigger than they were.

CLEAR NIGHTS

The moon
like a knife.
The bay, breathing,
the town asleep along the shore
except for the elongated shriek
of a Chevy at the edge of town
laying a strip a mile long,
black on black.
Somebody's signature.
Clear nights
and the moon looks down
as if it expects something.
Even in a town with nothing to do,
the fifteen-year-old boys will think of something,
drinking or cars, they'll find a way
to compress their own daring,
though the moon conspiring
with the morning light
will always betray them,
turn their ache
into nothing.
Late night smelling of burnt rubber,
they go wandering,
together, apart,
through fields of bitter wild pears,
urinating into the sweet-sick smell of fallen apples,
tossing rocks,
heaving rain-shaped bricks through the window
of a lost cabin, huge mossy beams
collapsed in a criss-cross of moonlight,
looking to flush out whatever still hides there,
snake or porcupine.
So little evidence
of those who came first.   Sometimes
only a pair of lilacs
planted in empty space
where the door would have been, lilacs
that flicker and blow out, spring upon winter,
year by year, the lavender flare
meaning welcome,
here at last, our own front door, the first settlers.
And then the land wouldn't give.
Fields constellated with rockpiles,
just as they left them, prepared for planting.

But the land would keep sloughing its scales
like an immortal snake,
rocks rising endlessly to the ground.
And now these small monuments of stones
look out with the grey eyes of the past.
Winter temples.   Under moonlight the cattle
with faces of wool,
pink rubbery muzzles
erasing the grass from the fields,
look up from their ungainly bulk with pink-rimmed eyes
as if each one weighed a ton and the whole ton ached,
yet watch how they back away
as a few spindly teenage boys
go toward them grinning,
no gun, no knife,
just a circular revenge they aren't
aware of, like coming down with some
sickness, biting down hard on this
violence between the teeth.

STARFISH

Through the rows of glasses a forsaken
streak of light, as on the solitary spoons
the gleaming strokes —
when sisters and brothers meet
in a dark bar at ten in the
morning after many years,
when the initiates of a family come together in the extreme
obscurity of their likenesses,
the closest friends
become bystanders.
The distances we've just come
to be together
would have taken some explorer's lifetime.

Irish coffees at ten in the morning:
cool rind of cream on the lip and the bitter whiskey beneath
whatever we talk about.
Whatever our friends fell in love with in each of us alone
is fraudulent.   Whenever we're together it seems
there's an eye loose here, a gesture there, and out of every sentence
one syllable we all pronounce the same.   As though between us
there is only one
child of our parents, whom we haunt and share.

There are sea anemones that by touch distinguish their own
from the others, and carefully do away
with the others.
There are single cells that choose to live in one
undulating raft
to navigate, synchronously, the waves.

All day we walk among the shops with their identical items.
And stand looking a long time
at what we know by heart.
The Golden Gate in fog.
The Golden Gate in sunshine
the color of rust, not golden at all.
Of all who jumped or meant to jump,
of all who meant to drown,
most leapt toward the harbor,
the city in their eyes.
Along the dock supports at waterline,
half in half out, the large pink starfish
neither crawling up
nor letting go.   Just grasping.
Large pink hands which are nobody's.

INTERMITTENT RAIN

Rain hitting the shovel
leaned against the house,
rain eating the edges
of the metal in tiny bites,
bloating the handle
so it will crack.
The rain quits and starts again.

There are people who go into that room in the house
where the piano is and close the door.
They play to get at that thing
on the tip of the tongue,
the thing they think of first and never say.
They would leave it out in the rain if they could.

The heart is a shovel leaning against a house somewhere
among the other forgotten tools.
The heart, it's always digging up old ground,
always wanting to give things a decent burial.

But so much stays fugitive,
inside,
where it can't be reached.

The piano is a way of practicing
speech when you have no mouth.
When the heart is a shovel that would bury itself.
Still we can go up casually to a piano
and sit down and start playing
the way the rain felt in someone else's bones
a hundred years ago,
before we were born,
before we were even one cell,
when the world was clean,
when there were no hearts or people,
the way it sounded
a billion years ago, pattering
into unknown ground.

Rain hitting the shovel
leaned against the house,
rain eating the edges of the metal.
The rain quits and starts again.

PROGNOSTICATIONS, HIGHWAY 27

Blue fog streaming
from warehouse windows,
the rest is blackness is trees,
heading south, Highway 27, southern Ontario.
Seen from above
we night-travellers must look
like lobsters brushing glowing feelers as we pass,
disturbing dust
on the ocean floor.
Getting it across:
the sense of shift.
The line between what you think and what you say.
That other line, between
what you say and what others say.
Resorting to your own uniqueness.   Reverting
to the use of unheard figures of speech.
Like certain birds who won't return
to the nest if the nest's been touched.
People are still wasting time beginning
sentences they know the end of.
This century will do away with the concept of greatness.

MARILYN BOWERING

LEAVETAKING

Language says: anything is possible,
all thoughts and loves can be,
all lost births.
Once I wanted twelve children, fair and dark,

but they were given to chance
which takes all. Some years were saved

that you might know
how I desired you.

If there is one
whom I trust, it is you.
Like truth you appeared
and vanished
in a company of angels.

No announcement came,
but someday
there will be a story.

Your room is decorated with ivory,
an animal skin spreads like a map of your youth —

that you know other names than mine

is neither sad nor insignificant:
the interior holds my attention.
I am not entranced,
there is no enchantment
broken —
our only mistake was time.

At any moment language abandons camouflage
and describes the world clearly:
you embrace it like snow drifting over
a winter night.

One more leavetaking and memory of you falters.

Achievement is all I ask:
that the words be your due.

THE ORIGIN OF SPECIES:
STARTING POINT

Let's say that the god's voice
is genuine;
that is, the brain is truly enlightened
by thoughts of it;

and that the brain is also an animal.

Let's say that they meet
at a cave entrance
neither possesses,

and further, that neither is strong:

understand that I mean there is no good
or evil.

But let's say that life is extinguished through conflict
and, in time, is resurrected (as is so),

and that the brain betrays understanding
in a story:

it loves and tames the bull-headed monster at its centre,

and all convolutions and laminae are taken-up
with death, sacrifice and honour,

and the white and grey matter are characters,
male and female, full of grace and beauty.

At such a moment I chose you.
At such a moment there was no god or animal.

Why not now? Why not always?

GAINS AND LOSSES

Winter pears, green and hard as ovaries,
were stored on the back porch.
Perhaps that is where
the women produced them, ready-made
from the womb.

Instead of babies
let us have fruit that can be kept quiet,
and eaten when required.

I am trying to tell the story:
how I found three infant mounds
and the wooden cross that grandpa made,
at Brookside: Wilbert, Clifford, Thomas
were the names.

I am opposed
to the human orchard —
        flower and be touched
        ingest pollen and work on it
until something sweet buds and falls.

Every story comes back to its beginning:
friends move like shadows on a curtain,
and we are alone, despite the planning.

Through this ability to produce
something useful

and keep it in quantity
for a winter
when the wind
blows down the chimney
and thieves through the rooms,

children are stolen,

either in their own, or another's memory.

Let me give you an instance.
Daddy shared a bed with his brother Thomas,
Thomas died, and Daddy didn't.

Daddy grew numb with death:
having escaped it, he had the wisdom
to hate it.

Other brothers died of other things,

but he fathered me
out of this hurtful
habit of living.

BETWEEN HUMAN FORMS

Not to let the dream
slide out of you unexpectedly
is important:

when leaving the body
you must become something
between human forms.

Picture yourself as a head
hung round with a necklace of smaller heads.
All of their mouths are open —
some have evil tongues.

If a dream enters one of these
your task is to behave well.
Meet and talk with others.

When the man touches,
when the woman touches back,
they are a necklace of heads whose tongues
never stop.

The first taboo is
silence.
The second taboo is
speech.

You must know which
can cause pain or prevent it.
You must not cause pain you cannot heal.
The man and woman are skilled
with each other.

That is their taboo.

THIS IS THE LAST TIME

This is the last time I can tell you,
but how can you believe me?

Never have we been so far apart.
Even the crying has stopped.

As long as you were with me
I had everything.
Why then the separation?
What bitterness can defeat love?

The sadness of centuries fills me.

It was a poison seed we grew,
and it has taken all rest,
all gentleness.

I can hardly believe the loss.

To think that a single life breaks
into a thousand,
that this seed we are born with and of
is stronger than us.

The ground became fertile for it.
Was that my idle thoughts' doing?

I could cut out both our hearts
to rid the world of this false paraclete
of self:

but then,

it is already done.

GIVING BACK DIAMONDS

Here's one:
I love you forever,

and another:
there's no one like you,

and another:
I'd do anything for you,

and the fourth:
I want you just as you are,

and the fifth:
goodbye forever, goodbye;

and you don't,
and though there isn't
and you don't,

no you don't,
you don't.

I love you forever
there's no one like you
I'd do anything for you
I want you just as you are
goodbye forever, goodbye

LEARNING THE BOMB

In the school-hall
rows of children crouch,
arms clutched over their heads,
learning the Bomb.

Will there be time to cross the field
(fire grappling at clothing,
stumbled by wind),
will there be time to get home,
and what if there are only children
to huddle each other
in the unprepared cellar?

Open the window
and see;
there are fires,
predictable as genii,
all over the city.

Open the window,
and a siren rivers down the street.

We watch with eyes
burrowed by a thousand species.

We still have something:
an occasional fire of the skin,
an amnesia of gentle hands
in a dark with no surname;

but what now,
when we find ourselves
children,
unnamed,
unforgiving?

MY WITNESS
a found poem from Bishop Witlock

The report on the other side
carries a message to all who can receive it:
no food supplements,
no special diets,
no medications,
laxatives,
exercises —
nothing which man can do was used to implement
His work in the prayer closet.

God has confirmed *His* word with the fruit, as reported.
Now I am not the only one...

I had reached a state of mental, physical and emotional
deterioration which caused me to cry out to God:
"Will you please take over."

By 1952 he had led me into the knowledge of prayer closet
travail.
I was healed of eye trouble,
migraines,
hemorrhoids,
sexual failure,
nerve torment;

cancerous type growths on my body were replaced by new skin.

Many personality changes have come to pass.

I asked the Lord why otherwise intelligent men and women
refuse to believe the evidence of 19 centuries.
He located the 'seat' of the Dragon in each person's physical
being.

He showed us the location in the head
and taught us the mind ulcers which Satan produces.

Ulcer one contains the thought which drives *To Possess*.
Ulcer two drives *To Use*,
and Ulcer three drives *To Remove* or *Replace* by extermination.
Murder.

The Spirit of God makes the difference,
delivers from all fear, hate sorrow, lust,
all iniquity,
all evil spirits.

Hallelujah!

THE MYSTERIES

I've been emptied:
interrogation, examination, evidence —
there's nothing left.
If there was a crime,
it's solved.
As for punishment —
no more starting towards the unknown
on a fresh horse,
and no choices as to path;

but to get out of the wind.

The casual gods have retired to heaven.
The Past and Future — that narrative that questioned,
falls silent.

Hollow flesh and bone have no resonance.

Dutifully, I move through the house
murmuring:
Who is the drowning man?
Why doesn't the swimmer
or boatman save him?
Why do they all go down?

Quietly. Quietly. Or words chasm open
crying — Lot, Avenge Your Children!

And beyond all, nodding as though they knew
but were keeping it back,
are the Mysteries,
the Chorus *castrati*,
guessing, as to the end.

LUCIA, MARTYR

At midnight,
when the inconstant pilgrims
sleep,
the old woman comes
and lifts the lid
of my coffin.

Her kiss is sunken
and warm,
not like my father's
which recalls
speechless death.

She loosens the shutters,
and I hear water touch,
stone by stone,
along the succeeding shore.
Her tears are minutes.
My father cannot know:
he had no midwife.

She has wept with me
since the earliest nights,
when Christ was not
my comforter.

WOOD-CUTTING

1.   No wood smoke, just mist foaming;
and cottonwoods, black as wands, yellow as flame;
and alder turned pale as a finch's belly —

these, quick as sound, cross the valley.

Only over time do we understand the absence of animals:

deadfalls/thinnings/slash.

Four years ago the creek was high
and the salmon returned and at sunset leapt and fed
on magenta-iced air.

Mallards pass.

A salvager comes in a boat, breaking the uneven silhouette
of change: all quickness,
and a slow-pulsed waiting.

2.   Being left behind is the worst,
the others gone into the forest.
Begging to be taken, and then being
left behind:

why want what you can't have?
Isn't that a child's lesson?

I was blind and you found me,
I was deaf

and you told me stories
of animal killings:

the hides to be brought out of the forest,
the meat, ready for stews.

At dawn we broke apart:

you refused everything from the future.
Even the sun, reflected on cloud,
could not touch you —

you had been left behind in the night.

While I was deep in my body,
you were resisting burial.

All this killing, all this getting meat —
you hear winter snuffling in corners
and are afraid —

it is natural to feel this,

and to leave behind someone who wants to follow you,
even willingly,

even when they are willing,
you will not be drawn into helpless harmony.

THE SUNDAY BEFORE WINTER

Though not always, today cloud blanks out distance.
Memory deepens the isolation.

This love is no comfort:

night and silence double,
though true evil blunts itself on the mettle of two.

There are few links in the life of the mind
between the dreamer and his island.
We are asleep, or awaken full of longing,
and so sleep and long
until life is a tract of absence.

I will not go under its anaesthetic
(unless you permit it).
Your touch is an anodyne of trust —

this is the certainty I swim or drown in —

as the moon darkens at the perigee,

and we tell hours
in death and repayment,
invalid as a moment.

Love, life, and will
are tempered by diminishing heat,

and utter, utter annexation.

EIDER DUCKS ON NOVEMBER BAY

The healing of our dissevered natures
is by finding each his proper mate:

each longing is happiness,
so the eider ducks call
when they land —

come
come
why do you avoid me
why do you avoid me —

and embrace in clear water, twinned
with the current
of eyes
of your pain.

Come
come
to possess
and not to possess;

will remain true to you
will remain

(every woodland and burning inlaid with moon-silver,
one says to another —
better not/to possess/to rejoice),

(the wind makes them mad,
tides
make the whole
that never was),

will remain true to you
why do you avoid me
come.

JAN CONN

SOUTH
for Susan Glickman

all winter the lake was a mirage:
the waves galloped white as horses
and the blue-green water was only
the tip of an iceberg.
the submerged part was where
I really lived —

south of Mexico, the hot yellow waist
of a continent, sensuous pink
of antheriums, the riot of greens
that play tricks on the eyes,
making you believe
the colours could feed you.

when I was fourteen, I was captured
by the Incas, and flew through Cuzco
on a giant green-feathered bird,
killing the Spaniards with poison
from a blow-gun. but I couldn't save the Indians,

and they dissolved in the desert,
leaving their marvellous temples
mesmerized by the sun.

I am one end of a long invisible cord
stretching between Toronto and these endless
green plains of sugar, coffee fincas, bunches
of bananas like fleet of tiny yellow boats,
moored by fabulous purple flowers, and needing
no sails, only a body of water stretching
thousands of miles, a compass, the will
to let everything go.

Dorothy and Bob Hargreaves' *Tropical Trees*
doesn't mention sapodilla, a metal-hard wood
the Mayans used for beams and lintels
to support their ceremonial centres.

no one could have told them termites
would one day collapse the eternal wood,
and all the limestone, reduced to cement
by burning, would form a substrate again
for the plants and trees covering
the Yucatán in a slow silent dream.

IN A BLACK WIND

last night I talked to you in Toronto.
I was crouched in the courtyard
where a wind was picking up
a few last rain drops and dusty
papaya leaves and driving them
against a white plaster wall.

this was the day of the Festival of Soldiers,
and military planes flew low overhead
celebrating more than a year in power
without a successful coup. you asked me
what I was thinking.

last week in Panajachel I heard
the firing squad, wanting to believe
in firecrackers. in the morning,
a man was dead in the street.
the children said

he had shiny shoes. red hibiscus
fell during the night on his dark shirt
and hair. someone dragged him
down a dirt road by his heels.

what is there to say. the mist lifted
from the lake and became the clouds
that drowned the mountains. I went
down to the shore to wash my hands.

they came out as black as the road
to the north in the Popul Vuh
or all the bars on windows
behind which faces are peering out,
faces that are slowly flickering out
like candles in a black wind.

FIFTEEN

a young girl, just fifteen.
jeans, sneakers, blue shirt.
climbs the slender poplar
at the end of a dark cedar hedge,
up through a sea of pale green light,
surfaces in the sun. warm raw air
smelling of things she doesn't yet understand.

she has come here to feel safe,
to survey her old kingdom —
the gulley, laced with straggling brambles
and clumps of brush, dead-man's-shack
covered with rust she pretended was blood,
and flowers in the dusty fields
so sweet they made her dizzy.

it doesn't belong to her anymore,
or she to it. she sees past it
to the low blue hills that make
some place inside her tense up.
she's not quite ready for their
expansiveness and the way they
diminish south and west
like puddles drying out at noon.

she says she may never leave,
then looks toward the large white house —
walls fold around her arms
and the doors slam shut as though
they might never open for her again.

she finds out no one is ever ready —
they just go ahead, or stand
in one place until the ground heaves
beneath them and they find out
they've moved anyway.

she thinks she'd rather move herself
but still sits motionless through
the long hot afternoon, inhaling
the sickly sweet smells, watching bees
crawl drunkenly out of the blossoms,
pretending she can stay, knowing
she'll leave this town
with the first person who asks.

FIRST LINES

she's under an umbrella, waiting
beside a maroon-coloured car.
it's one of her first real dates,
so she's early, she's always early
for things. she's sure her watch
has stopped; she checks it the way
some people check their pulse.

this rain, and the low sheep-like clouds
hanging, dripping, on her shoes,
on her new dress, obscure the street,
the car, people emerge from mist
a little way from her like fog-bound
boats, swell by, and vanish
taking the sensation of wet rain on skin
and damp vegetation with them.

it seems to her she's been hanging around
for hours, she keeps licking her lips,
letting them dry, wetting them.
she thinks they're hers. they could
belong to anyone, if they asked.
it's not that she's an easy lay, it's
just she's learned to try to please
them, the young men, and they know
what they want.

they want the slight tremor in the
lower lip, the open space on the forehead
where no expression has really settled
before. they aren't cruel, they just want
to put the first lines in.

WHILE I WAS LOOKING AT THE BACKGROUND
YOU WALKED OUT OF THE PICTURE

I don't know why I chose
to send you a tiger: it stands
so still, bright in the shadows
of tropical trees. plants around it
send up volleys of smells, exotic,
fantastic. the night is dark, the tiger

radiant. fur burns intense orange,
eyes the colour of a harvest
moon, the one I saw last time

I was with you. ears filled with
white hair like a thousand moth antennae
bent in, listening to dreams

of the forest. night sounds: frogs
creaking and insects crackling
like pine cones on fire. sometimes
a bird or a small animal rustling.

you used to travel then — India,
Africa, Colombia — and left me
behind, always, coming home months later
with another smell on your skin,
the suitcase of saris and ivory
elephants for your wife, small gifts
for us, the daughters, growing like
Hallowe'en pumpkins, awkward teeth
in our grins. once I wanted to be
an archaeologist, to go where you'd
been, while the scent was still fresh.

FOOTFALLS IN THE DUSK

an echo, a shadow, footfalls
in the dusk. perhaps it would
be better if we were born blind.
moonlight splashes on grass
cut short as a crewcut.
the blades gleam like small swords
battling the blacked-out memories
of stars. the tension between us
taut as a harp string.
one pluck and the whole sky
would ignite. so I don't touch you.

we lie on this moist grass
as though on a bed of nails.
a hundred pinprick holes
when we stand up, the blood
invisible. I cannot tell you
how long I have waited
for your breath to still.

around us, trees unbolt
green cloth; peel off layers
of grey bark. the holes in the universe
are not black, they are only
the absence of all known things.

your pulse flutters,
a whisper of dried leaves
turning cartwheels in the wind.
clouds flee to their dawn address.
we go home stepping
on splinters of light.

ORANGE LIGHT IN APRIL

sunlight spills down like
crates of mandarins upended,
bruising my arms and sending
points of orange light
into my eyes. the wind today
is an April wind.

flocks of newspapers sail
over brown grass, collect
at streetcorners and in soggy parks
as though they were on their way
somewhere, their black & white lungs
fluttering vainly, trying to fly or run.

you appear in the crowd
like a blue fragment of sky,
walking toward me, thinking
I can't ever know what.
it is always these times when
maples and beech lean greyly
into the afternoon that I wish
I could tell you
how much the sight of you
simply striding in an element
you have made yours, amazes me.

even inside the warm panelled room,
surrounded by stained glass,
attended by white linen,
I can barely look at you.
I think you would see straight
through me, an x-ray of the heart,
perceive desire & need,
and turn away from it.

CHOICES

the falls spill over grey walls of rock,
a repeated hallucination. marble green water
unfurls white crinolines of foam that
cascade over the edge like five thousand
angels in anklets of lace.

churning in the river's jaw
like loosened teeth, chunks of ice
jostle each other near the lip
of boiling water, then grind
and shatter far below.

once a man crossed this on a tightrope —
others rolled over in barrels. some
survived, some dreamed over and over
white water caught in the grapes of their lungs.

last year a woman dropped her child
over the black rail. was slow
to scream for help. exposure
takes too long, she said.

all night the child's fingers
climbed the bedroom walls
like the knuckles of spiders.
the mother bathed in moonwater,
wanted to live in the mouth of a rose.
the child was an octopus, hungry
for love or milk. she provided milk.
love was a luxury.

we walk between twisted trees,
make starts of conversation.
wind whips sheets of snow
over dead grass; pares our faces
thin as paper.

we lean over the rails, stare down
until the water shifts, begins to fall
up. spray beads our hands, we reel
like drunken boats. we're not yet sure
why we're here. a sign nearby says
keep back. it doesn't say
don't jump.

CARDINAL

it has just rained. a light, clear rain
you could walk in for hours, and never
get really wet. you're in the backyard,
inhaling the fresh green smell of flowers,
up on your toes, hoping for... what?

a cardinal lands on a branch, a black
branch that's just been rained on. it gleams,
wetly, it's like a little black river.
the bird an explosion of crimson,
a firecracker. a fistful of feathers
clutched around a tiny heart.
what could possibly hold it together?

its song makes you want to leave
your body stranded in the grass,
but you don't know how. this isn't
a dream, and you can't shrug it off
like a shirt.

magnolia blossoms dazzle you, they swell up
twice their size, inhaling damp air.
the green of new leaves so wild and rich
you think you could live off it, you'd like
sap to swim through your veins, not blood.

a gull swoops down low then goes out
over the water, straight south. it's hazy,
with all this rain, and you can't quite
make out the other side.

there are patches of grey on the lake
that look almost solid, like stepping stones.
you think you'll follow them later,
when you have more time. when do you first
notice, you don't have more time.

RED SHOES IN THE RAIN

you have been here three days.
just long enough to leave
yourself in every corner
of the house — leaning against
dusky pink walls with your arms
folded lightly across your chest
or behind your head, waiting for someone
as though you were still at the airport
or in some crowded railway station
in another city.

the coat in the closet holds your shape.
it could almost glide out the door
on its own, shrug its shoulders,
pull away from me wanting
to keep it here.

you have gone out — to be alone,
to concentrate on other things.
while I stare and stare at
slate-blue water and black trees
dancing three inches off the ground.

the house has never been so empty.
your presence leaks out like oxygen
under the door, out the windows,
follows you down the street like a spy.

there is not enough time to say
all the things that crowd up, images
swelling and vanishing with each breath.

soon you'll be gone again. each time
the gap widens slightly as though
a river was flooding its banks
and we were on either side, shivering,
taking turns lighting smouldering fires.
signals. we stand and wave; put back on
our separate lives that wait like
a pair of red shoes left out all night
in the rain. it's no good. they've
shrunken. they'll never fit the same way again.

INSTRUCTIONS TO A DAUGHTER

I

hold nothing in the hands
that cannot be fused to itself:
molten metal, the white petals of cells,
a fistful of snow melting.
do not speak. make the words
form themselves in the bones
of the skull and clatter against
the tongue's roof. then send them out
letter by letter with a bow
made from the tendons of the heart.

do this once a year for ten years.
come back and I will teach you to sing
like wind hidden in fig flowers, like
minerals ascending pine tasting
light and air for the first time,
like the vertebrae of a whale, like mountains
pulsing in a summer storm.

II

burn the heart like a wick in oil.
pluck it out: hold it so
the four winds can breathe on it;
cover it with ashes from a wood fire,
disguise it as a fist, wrap it
in a palm leaf.

let no one watch as you offer
it to the hawk from the east,
the egret to the west, the parrot
of the south, the pigeon from
the north. they will each take
one chamber and fly for three days
to the four edges of the world.

then they will call to you and
you will hear them first with
your feet, then your thighs,
then the empty cage of the ribs.
you must answer them all making
a sound as of oars dipping
in deep water and then you must
find the four pieces of the heart
and sew them together with string
made of straw. then you will be ready
to learn how to love.

WHEN WE BEGIN TO BURN

what can I learn about your childhood
in the Similkameen from the inside
of an office in a grey stone building
in Toronto? you collected wildflowers and
mushrooms, ended up a biologist.
no one was surprised.

as a boy you spent hours perched on
hillsides, looking down — imagined
being alive before the dinosaurs.
all the layers of rock — rust and buff,
with thin streaks of metal like gold thread
running through a silk blouse, and the
sagebrush making dry heat, the dust
reducing everything to dull brown & grey.

thin arms resembling broomsticks,
you became an airplane, a bush pilot
who rescued men lost on ice floes
in the unexplored north. I went south
disguised as Huckleberry Finn,
followed my father. he never recognized me.

in what I know of you and high school
there's a gap. I want to hear about
the man you fell in love with
after your girlfriend moved
away from town.

I had just met someone who would
leave me in a bar in Montreal,
who painted fantasies I couldn't
believe, who knew too much, who
overwhelmed me.

the leaves were turning, the colours
leaked into my skin. I was transparent,
glided inches off the ground,
even learned to walk through walls.
I remember hoping

there was a clearing someplace
beneath dark green pine like the one
you and your lover lay in. I imagined
the last wildflowers blooming with a
romantic brilliance, but you say

fall in these mountains isn't like
that, it's a time of small soft
colours, of fungi and dying grasses.

it was I who wore a mustache to the
costume party. you don't pretend
anything, the blue and white kimono
flows down your slender frame,
a waterfall when you move.

the woman dressed as Othello
knows exactly where she fits.
the deep sea diver asks you to dance,
he isn't prepared for a yes.

I'm addicted to this kind of ambiguity,
no easy answers. the devil asks
if we're men or women. we bow and answer
in Japanese, whisper into our sleeves.

we make a black plastic bat circle its
white nylon string, we want to fly
that much. we tell the devil we'd
sell our souls for a pair of wings.
like Icarus, we're learning to soar.
there'll be no one to catch us
when we begin to burn.

LORNA CROZIER

MONOLOGUE: PRISONER WITHOUT A NAME

Blindfolded,
you can't see who beats you.
It could be someone you called friend.
It could be your neighbour, or
the woman you saw buying bread,
the one who returned your smile
as she tapped the crust with her finger.

Sometimes there are voices far below
the pain. You hear about their children,
how one's son is failing school,
how another's daughter is growing beautiful.
You hear about the rising cost of things,
about the suppers that await them
in their houses on the other side
of town.

When all you have is pain and darkness
time stretches ahead like a desert
you can't walk out of, a desert
in a dream you cannot touch.
There is no reference point,
in two hours, tomorrow — these are things
you can't say, you don't know them anymore.

The first temptation is suicide
then madness.

But one day you choose to survive.
You eat your food, the same food,
but you eat it differently.
You listen for rain on the roof, for wind.
You imagine wind in a woman's hair.

You sense when the one who beats you
is nervous
when he doesn't want to kill.

And so when you leave,
if they let you go,
there is something left of you
like a pebble you have hidden
all these months in your pocket,
a pebble you've polished in the darkness
behind the blindfold, bringing out its colours,
its shy designs.

And if you are lucky,
if this is a lucky stone, let's say,

you can push away the bitterness
and there is room for soemthing else,
another feeling, perhaps something
close to love.

PAVLOVA

Even you, Pavolova, you
with the beautiful feet and arms,
even you did not die
with grace or beauty.
Your last words
Get my swan costume ready
were what we would have written
for you, but death would not
lift you weightless
into the bright air.

You waited
in the shadows of the wings,
moistening your lips,
crossing yourself as you had
a hundred times before.
Should I have had children instead?
Sons and daughters
to show pictures to.
This is the country I left,
see why I weep.

In Russia the snow is falling
as it does in memory, falling
from the backs of horses,
settling in the furs of women
who ride to the concert halls.
In your garden in England
the swan who laid his neck
across your shoulders
and bit your flesh
in his dark unpredictable beak
dreams himself whole again
up to where the sky
was made for swans.

Lonely and sick you lie
in a Dutch hotel.
Your lungs like stones
press you into the bed.
Your fingers clutching your husband's hand
feel the warmth of the mistress
he left just moments ago.
You hear his words
She will not dance tomorrow,
as the doctor cuts
into your ribs
to drain the pus
and let the breath in.

MID-FEBRUARY

Outside the grey sky
falls and continues to fall
around your muffled body
that bends, straightens, bends,
your dull blade bruising wood.

In the frame of the kitchen window
a bird lights on the dying elm.
Its breast is bright, yellow
as the three chrysanthemums
you brought home yesterday
wrapped in tissue and waxed paper
green as growing.

Through flowers I watch
your red mitts following
the axe, the image of the bird
held in glass. I cup
the colours to my eyes
to wash away the hours
when I couldn't show my care
or feel the simple joy
of flowers and a bird.

As you pile wood
in the crook of your arm,
the bird stretches its wings.
Up from the warm throat
its song rises in the snow,
in the slow heart.

ANCESTRY

for Sarah and Eli

Sarah the young one
born in the city
sees her father's
murderer thumb, his killer eye
In Toronto he confesses
     It was the wind
     when I left the prairie
     I pulled it from the sky
     buried it
     like a grandfather
     you have never seen

That summer they return
to the graves of his ancestors
Her father walks among stones
among gravehouses, reads aloud
the Hebraic letters
writes them down in books

Sarah finds the marker
washed nameless by rain
unearths the old bones
scrapes them clean
with a xyster zt zt zt
draws a mouth on the skull
Already she sees
the grasses move
feels invisible
fingers ruffle her hair

In a paper bag
she carries them
back to the city
strings them together
hangs them in her window
At night they chime
the names of all her dead
and what they have seen of the dark
wind in the marrow
wind in the heart

THIS IS A LOVE POEM WITHOUT RESTRAINT

It wants to say
heart. It wants
to say trust
It wants to say
forever   forever
forever

What are you going to do about it?
You cannot stop me
now

.

It will talk
of beauty
Lilacs   Apples
The smell of rain
in caraganas
Your mouth
your eyes

.

This poem
is full of pain
full of pieces
It cries out
oh! oh! oh!
It has no pride
no discretion
It whimpers
It will not drop its eyes
when it meets a stranger
It will not hide
its tears

.

The moon shines
on this page
as the poem writes
itself.   It is trying
to find whiteness
frost on snow
two feathers
on a pillow
your hands
            upon
my skin

•

These words are tired
of being
            words
They refuse to sit here
pretending
            they can't move
                        off the page

These are the first
ones to leave
their white space
They fall
on your tongue
letter by letter
like raindrops

One of them
is my name
What will you do with it?
It has decided to live
inside you

•

This poem has no restraint
It will not say
plum blossom
sunset
rubbing stone
cat's cradle

It refuses to be
evasive

I miss you
I miss you
Come home

•

It won't talk of passion
but the sleep that follows
when our bodies
touch

That moment just
before waking
when we realize
we've been holding one another
in our sleep

•

How do you use the word *love*
in a poem?
Love.

If you stare at it
long enough
it will burn into your eyes
and last

•

THE LAST DAY OF FALL
for Howie White

The wind cold, the cold
wind bringing in tomorrow's frost.
Flower beds dug up, the soil turned
 and in the yellow grass that was not out
in the last few days of growing, a bird
hunches, then hops lopsided away;
bird with one wing dragging, beautiful
russet breast, a beak to gather seeds.

The last sweet moments of fall
we wanted to gather in, bright leaves
to carry us through the winter.
Instead a broken bird at our feet
and what's to be done?
Let it die slowly in a box or cage?
Kill it here? This is the last day
of fall. In nights that grow longer
a bird will drag its wing across our eyes.

Somewhere there is a man
who can kill. Neither of us can
strike it with a stone or crush
its skull with our heels.
We turn away, leave it in the grass.
Here there are seeds, we say,
the euthanasia of early snow
the quick mercy
of a cat.

THERE ARE LIMITS

He has a present for me,
something he caught
this morning in Echo Lake.
I think of the lure,
the dead eyes.
A fish? I ask.
Better than that, he replies,
pulling from his pocket
a piece of glass
shaped like a fish.

*It is a dream
the glass had.*
He presses it into my palm,
tells me he'll stop
thinking of me now.
He has reeled in
his line, the fish
is made of glass.
*Life is not what we thought,
there are limits
to loving.*

I hang the glass
in my kitchen window.
It turns and turns
tangling the sunlight.
Echoes of fish
flicker on the walls.

This is better than a word,
better than a promise.
There are limits to weeping.
It is a dream
my tears have had.
They turn into fish
brittle as glass.

MARY DI MICHELE

LOVE SCENES

Light in the late afternoon,
dressed to be savoured,
as dry as white vermouth
with a twist of lemon,
the park we frequent,
an oasis of air,
free for its running stretches,
after the constriction of row housing,
high rise apartments, bank towers,
it trips into cool maples,
blesses slides, swings, sand boxes,
the sun kissed knees of children,
in a park dedicated to Sibelius,
his head on display on a slab,
a queer turquoise brow
posing on a black monolith.
Between the playground
and the baseball diamond,
music, sentenced like an unruly child
to a corner,
like a benched player
exiled from the game.

Before the dinner hour
love is a dry martini,
part distilled liquor,
part an aged wine,
it invests too much sugar
in the blood,
the olive with its pit,
small memento of lost lovers,
the aftertaste of oil,
smooth squeak of its flesh
against your teeth,
the unwholesome green
of some romantic poet's
lovesickness,
degrader of sonnets,
a pit so like the small stones
the body forms out of its pain,
deposited in the gall bladder
or the kidneys.

A toddler's stride can
make a marathon of a mile,
plodding up a round hill,
legs wide apart,

arms clipping paper dolls out of air,
the space she's just been,
her centre of gravity so close to earth
she picks up some of her speed
from the rotation of the planet,

chasing pigeons, those slow fat city birds,
glutted on chewed up bits of arrowroot biscuit,
bubbles of popcorn, crusts of white bread,
chickens she calls them and when corrected
the best she can manage is "kitgeons",
imagination or the lack of all her teeth
transforming the park into a coop,
the sudden clapping of wings
audience to her wonder.

Vigilant in her care,
the mother is all
the child will ever experience
of guardian angels.

Her father minds her in his heart,
somewhere in Victoria,
but his story is here,
as immediate as a film image,
as remote,
he is audience to his own life,
he imagines a sheet of glass
as close,
as far away as he can come.
He flattens his nose against the window,
hands, clenched fists,
losing definition against the pane.
He is most lonely for himself.
Rain and tears
like water and wine
mix in a gold chalice,
he has given it all up:
what's most precious to him,
like Stella Dallas watching
secretly through a window,
that upper class twit of a father,
giving the bride away,
Stella locked out in the weather
from the cathedral and social whirr
her shop girl accent is anathema to.

Barbara Stanwyck, you stupid bitch,
I liked you better as the matriarch
in the Big Valley on TV

or the gun moll who gave Gary Cooper
such an interesting time.
There are so many women like you,
who think pathos their prerogative,
under your clothes,
more clothes,
unfeeling mannequins made
of wire hangers and papier mâché.
A man could strike a match
and walk away with a clear conscience.

Imperceptible how
guilt resembles resentment
in the mind,
the subtly changing shapes
in a landscape devised by Escher,
that dress of Roo's
where the blue fish at the hem are
transformed into birds by the bodice.

He keeps an eye on her in the park
from his living room in another city.
He knows how she could play on the swings
for hours, her laughter in his lungs
is the thunder of blood
in a sparrow's flight,
the hollow bones built for light,
for speed, for vanishing into the blue.

He ends up squatting by a bed
of marigolds, tearing unconsciously
at the petals, awake all night
because of the perfume
of those catholic flowers
smelling of old shoes.

HUNGER

For some the afternoon light is a mess
of leftover porridge,
a greying, clotted mass,
to be eaten again for dinner,
or the rye that stains the bottom
of an unwashed glass.
A room with a 1000 walls is cramped.
A man can't take two steps
without running into a corner,
assaulted by tongues of peeling plaster,
dry chips and a fine white dust
shifting through the wool
any room makes of time and traffic.

A man loses his hand in the jungle
of the top drawer of his dresser.
He pulls out glossy pages
stiff with semen,
the legs of sex with
those glistening organs for sale
like fruit in pint boxes
exposed through plastic net.

Disguised as a child, a 24 year old model,
in Penthouse, December issue,
only partially clothed and provocative
poses in Buster Brown shoes and ankle socks.
Above her white pleated skirt,
the nipples of her bare breasts
are red cinnamon hearts.

A man opens a magazine and enters
the steaming and ruthless
rainforest of his origins,
something dry and slithering
coils and squeezes out every other
thought.
He flips through the pages and grows
a third and murderous arm.
He did not kill the pianist,
like that character in a late night
horror movie on TV,
who murders a musician to borrow
his hands and a talent
to perform in concerts
for all those who are attentive
in white linen, pearls, and furs.

There's appetite and then there's hunger.
Bob Guccione didn't intend his magazine
for the man employed in a sweat shop
on Spadina. Even a work horse knows this
as he barters with his boss
for the remnants of light
through basement windows,
barred, as if life itself
were a prison sentence.

Daily the only weather
he experiences through footwear.
With shoes he imagines
returning to a home filled
with bitching or laughter,
discovering his arms abundant with
the warmth and clean laundry smells
of a wife. Through her soft shirt he can feel
the three tiny hooks holding up her bra.
Bob Guccione designed his magazine for men
who are bored with this.

Sunday in the freezing rain,
March with its stranglehold on light,
a sun somehow more intimate,
more chilling. A child, a girl,
a female person, lingering in the park,
rubber boots squeaking,
kicking in the ice
in soft spots with her heels.

Lured by her pleated skirt,
by the flash of light
on her shiny black boots,
by her soft brown eyes,
turned inward and brooding,
he approaches when Sibelius
is the only witness,
and the disinterested blinds
of rooming house windows.

He is a man with large hands
and dry, unblinking eyes.

Hypnotized by his stare,
unable to scramble for even an idea
of escape,
lips quivering in the nightmare,

she silently calls to her mother.

In no time at all
his eyelashes must flutter
break the spell
so that she can wake
up and stop
herself from being pulled along,
where?

Breathless in plastic wrap:

she is dressed for outdoors
in the pleated skirt
her mother gave her for Christmas,
and a brown sweater, whose bulky knit,
camouflages her sex,
breasts a boy might have,
tender breasts,
pink and sweet as cinnamon hearts:

in a fridge, like a fetus folded
into that white space
where all dreams end
including this one
where she has been made to be
of man unborn.

NATURAL BEAUTY
for Roo

1

Post Santa Claus parade,
wake for November,
a few balloons
abandoned by children and clowns,
astray in gutters,
their purpose, vague
as deflated sexual organs.

Rot of dead leaves and autumnal rain,
reds and golds reduced
to a monochromatic rust,
more ash than leaf
they make a paste,
like soap scum and pubic hair
clogging bath drains.

Defoliated trees, unsexed,
such self mutilation a formal survival,
blocked on the avenue like the dead
bodies in the climax
of Shakespearean tragedy,
never without its comic element,
a brief speech in prose
delivered by two balloons,
lungs filled with yellow and mauve.

How did they get up there?
tied to the penultimate branch
of a lofty maple,
some squirrels' party?
a few last words in a silly charade:

Mime crocus, jonquil or narcissus.

2

The ugly city greets you,
the ugly city of little sky
and less earth,
where eyes must be adapted to see
teeming zoos in test tubes,
the garden hose and all it suggests
of sudden reptiles,
the bats like sly frisbees
returning to boys in twilight,
or fluttering up like dead leaves

reversing gravity to haunt
familiar branches,
the coons, hustlers,
I have to chase out the back door
naked except for my broom.

No mountains, no view,
no longer golden, the trees
like mannequins stripped,
the window dresser having split
for a long vacation in Acapulco.
Newspapers and the odd candy wrapper
neurotically tossed this way and that
by every breeze,
gossiping,
rubbing too many people
the wrong way.

Sky is downcast,
all colour drained from light
so that outdoor seems like indoor
radiation of fluorescent fixtures,
known to butcher brain cells,
suspected to put to sleep
feeling.

City living gives you an eye
for detail, the single tree,
a leaf of grass,
a sprig of camomile
pushing its way back up from the sneakers
of children,
all that is resilient in nature
and won't easily die
or like pigeons and sparrows
too plain to be killed.

This city misses you.
This city strains for meaning
as through the OED
with a magnifying glass.

   3

Something odd happened
on the way to meet you at the subway,
walking south on Spadina,
I stumbled across the startling
beauty of purple blossoms
radiating from a small bush,

a tropical array barely imaginable
in late November drizzle.

I wanted to pick a floret
not only to share this vision
but as a sort of evidence
for the fertile imagination
of some anonymous gardener
whose lyrical fingers had caused
some rare bush to skirl
in southern Ontario,
blowing in the neon colours of hydrangea
you regret from Vancouver days.

My fingers were stunned
when I tried to snap
off a blossom
to tear the rubbery sinew
of the plant,
as my brain slowly circulated
(sugar is the root of all knowledge)
recognition of a fake,
a plastic plant growing out of
urban ordure and dust.

4

Absence of beauty is a scar,
a harelip, a limp,
a wheelchair going nowhere
up and down ramps
of institutions.

Your absence is a fresh wound.

I could visit you in California
and become beautiful by association
in the same way as a woman
about to sing
will pin a white camellia
in her hair and croon
such silky, textured lyrics,
her own inner bud darkly flowering.

This is all of fashion I care to emulate.

Your landscape is mentholated,
eucalyptus and lemon
so fragrant it frees
all breathing passages.
In every corner of your home

fruit of a single tree
in the yard, persimmons ripen
to a jellied
lushness, too many for your puddings
and pies.

5

How does a woman the colour of earth
suggest so much of the sky?
By trusting to who she is?
by making all her conceits
metaphysical?

Proust believed original talent
like Beethoven's
creates its own audience,
so we learned to listen with the length of our bodies,
so that the circulation of blood, pulse,
rumbles and rhythms of internal organs,
mute transfers of chemicals between cells,
electric rushes through the brain,
are orchestrated with the sonatas
of that deaf man,
composing faster than the speed of sound.

Your face converted all my eyes.

I got to know it better
buried in the files
of Physics' purchasing office
at the U. of T. one summer.

Beauty, I was taught, at best,
a kind of intrigue,
mystery of madonnas, inaccessibility of virgins.
Beauty, I came to appreciate best,
a kind of incongruity:
Emily, as blonde as a daffodil
dressed in black for hallowe'en,
a witch in her fake sinister attire,
the Mio man delivering soda pop
with a rose between his teeth
when I was expecting Giorgio
another master in the art
of beauty as the unexpected.

It's the brew we have to acquire
a taste for, like whiskey or coffee,
that is most narcotic.

Roo who never in your life
spent so much as 10¢ on makeup,
look at all the colours that you are.
Alas, something constricts my throat
visualizing your visage
with its sweet melancholy of wisteria
and listening to your name, Roo:
Ruth, a mouth full of flowers,
Roo, a Sufi dish like roses diablo.

Romeo was wrong and Rilke was right,
much of the pleasure of the senses
is an incense in   the ear.
It's all sweeter, sweetest,
because of your name.

SUSAN GLICKMAN

ONE HAND CLAPPING

Some questions have no answers.
These are the ones we must ask.

How finds the way.
Why builds the road.

One travels light in darkness;
Two, both lighter and darker.

We are what the light makes
when it stops moving.

GARGOYLES

Sunlight in the window,
a cup of lemon tea.
Nothing is about to happen.
This moment is mine —
I hold it in my hand and say
Yes, this is a new day,
I don't believe we've met before,
then lean on my porch,
pretending to be a man in shirtsleeves, smoking,
or a grandmother resting her years.

I can feel myself fitting into the long corridors
of balcony-loungers all over the city:
we are the gargoyles of the great cathedral.
It is our scrutiny which brings pink
to geraniums, red to the tiles of the roof,
a vivid blue to the ribbons
in a little girl's hair.

It is our vigilance that fills the air
with breakfast smells, and the memory
of last night's rain. We are
the attentive ones, the guardians,
drinkers of tea
in the cup of the day.

HOME ON THE RANGE

"Loving you is no joke
            although it's funny as hell,"
my cowboy says,
        peering off at the horizon
    where the cavalry ought to appear
                        if they had any sense.
        "Uh huh,"
    I reply, engrossed in *Mary Worth*,
    where life
            is unfolding as it should
                one square at a time,
                        all the facts intact.

        The kid flings the paper
                on my porch each morning
    with all the negligence
        of youth. I collect the blown pages
            from the yard, recipes
        dangling from the shrubbery,
                the stock-market lodged
            behind a tree. My horoscope says not to get
carried away, to use
        my common sense.

                    This man
                isn't about to carry me off
                        anywhere:
        He wants a pair of pink arms to crawl into
                to wait out winter.
        Knowing this
            he is ashamed.
        Being ashamed
            he's looking for a fight.

I pour him some coffee, a safe domestic gesture,
        and try not to apply the headlines
        too literally to the day.
    "Gold is going up. Snow is coming down,"
            I venture,
                conversationally.
    I know how to avoid
                    an argument;
            I like my coffee hot.

SONG WITHOUT WORDS

There are too many things I don't have names for.
That's why I keep stopping in the middle of the street,
my heart buttoned in somebody's pocket,
or prowl the aisles of the Dominion store,
studying the hieroglyphics on the back
of a cereal box. I'm tired of finding the day
bundled on my doorstep in a hospital blanket:
not even a bit of ribbon for a token, a silver locket,
a bracelet of hair. Every night I have to bury it again
under the radiator with the sprung mousetrap
and hear it crying through the pipes. I lie in bed listening,
my feet as far away as India.

LIVING ALONE

Not such a hard thing to do
if you have the right appliances.
A radio is essential: that voice in the background
eases you into the day
like a breakfast egg into water.
For that, of course, you need a stove,
a pot, a spoon or two —
one of those beautifully turned pepper-mills, preferably teak.

If you stay in the kitchen it's amazing how much space
you can fill:
a coffee-grinder, blender, garlic press,
all manner of intricate knife.
Emergency rations: instead of baked beans
smoked oysters, a bottle of brandy.

These things taste best at 2 a.m.
when the rest of the house is cold.
You wake up dreaming you're asleep in the fridge,
there's so much white space beside you.

UNDERGROUND

We're always moving forward by half-measures, afraid
to risk too much: standing rigid on the escalator, unable to look
at those passing the other way. Always something
in our arms — purses, briefcases, paper bags —
for the same reason we keep our clothes on,
to feel something around us.

But where are they going, those other travellers?
Sitting across from them on the subway
we deduce a life from dentures,
from worn shoes and wedding rings.
Right thumb and forefinger screw the ring 'round and 'round
like the lid on a child-proof bottle.

If a drunk staggers on, or someone starts crying,
there's a moment's reprieve.
Eyes slide together
furtive as lovers under a bush
but still nobody speaks. Words
would choke like pure oxygen here, underground.

But the drunk spills out his story, insatiate;
the girl keeps on crying. Sometimes
you've got to make a mess.
At the asylum I worked in — those women
who smeared shit on the walls,
they weren't being dirty,
they just wanted to learn to paint.

PASSING WORDS
for Dennis Lee

Nothing is easy, that's what we're all saying,
the bruised lovers finding a laugh at the back
of anguish, the baffled parents stuttering over how, how,
to say anything true
to the small ones whose nightmares are less frightening
that the world they wake to;
all of us numb over machines whose noise cannot crowd out
the problems we go home to.
Trying to keep things clear. Trying to keep headlines
out of kitchens, to keep cancer from soup and bread,
bombs out of the bedroom. These
only the big ones
the ones so big they can't be seen; fiery stars
obscured by daylight and the atmosphere of earth
that startle us when night draws back
its curtains.
Usually it's the ordinary problems that won't let go,
that heckle and jeer behind day's little triumphs —
failure of work, failure of play, failure
of love. But we all keep going, nothing
is easy we say, we say it
so easily.

THE SADNESS OF MOTHERS

The greatest poverty of all is this —
to live for the joy
of others; to never know, or always too late
what could possibly gladden oneself. This
is the sadness of mothers
and the continuing crime
of the world. And every child
perpetrates it
and every mother
is a willing victim
and it goes on and on, the pelican
suckling its young on its own blood,
the nightingale's chest against the thorn
singing the sweet song of martyrdom
to the greedy ear of the world. Oh,
the sadness of mothers haunts me, it fills my days
with lonely eyes, they are everywhere: pushing carriages
down alleys, back and forth in the hot sun,
sitting at bus-stops with too many packages
and not enough hands, never enough hands to wipe
all the tears of others, never enough hands
to wipe tears of their own
never enough hands   enough hearts   enough bosoms
to lay to rest the sadness of everyone but especially
the sadness of mothers. Mothers weeping for the lost dreams
of children and the indignities of men,
mothers weeping for the girls they were one summer
before the world closed in. The sadness of mothers
is everywhere and a great crime and no one
will pay for it and no one can.

NAMING THE DRAGONS

Always the same silence.
After nimble, defiant discussion of everything
else — two women in a room at night
inside the porcelain cup
of winter, two women working overtime
to understand their lives —
the word "men" hits the floor like a smoke bomb,
a grey perplexity in which we lose
our way.

If only the baby would cry now
to give us some focus.
If only we could arrive at some stop-gap summation
to let us quit the confessional
with grace.

There's never an easy way out
to know our dark brothers:
what they keep from themselves they also keep
from us. Night after night
we anatomize ourselves
looking for Adam's rib, the thing they fear they've lost
by giving themselves to us.

How we confront that fear in them each time,
each time we hope to fearlessly
go on. How we stand over the torrent
watching the house wash away —
how there's never any bridge,
how we must learn to build one over and over again.

The things we thought were simple, bed and board,
shift their shapes in moonlight
to dragons of venom and steel.
Money and work, the monsters of everyday,
crawl tamely past like sensible household pets.

IL MONDO SENZA GENTE

for Sheldon Zitner

A pale green rain falls like pollen on the quiet streets.
I am reading a book;
its vast abstractions noble and remote
as mountains seen from a plane; mountains
no one ever skied down
or trudged up
at the rim of the habitable world.

The man whose book I'm reading speaks of *tragic form*
and I feel the requisite yearning, reduced to a pair
of suppliant marble arms.
It would be nice to be a statue,
to be that still.

Dante's "world without people".
No one I know is heroic,
or not for long. We never know when to stop —
how to freeze the revealing gesture
at the moment life spills its guts.

I know I am being stubborn; I know
the sentimentality of *the real*
can simplify as fatally
as art. For instance:

> *The light shifts*
> *in the window, and slides in grey*
> *and cold. It smells of hunger; it smells*
> *of dirty children*
> *and buildings falling down.*

But this resolves nothing.

TO PATAGONIA
for Jan Conn

My birthday amaryllis, sexual red and white,
delivered both stalks at once, eight trumpets sounding
in sequence. According to Cameron's copy of
Crockett's Victory Garden, it should have flowered twice,
gaudy blooms teasing me over breakfast
like the stamps on your letters from Guatemala City
or these hot winds from the ever-mysterious South.

South of here is only Niagara Falls; exotic enough
for first visitors to these shores
but now almost domestic, fenced in
by golden arches. But south, and south again,
you purchase stamps in the post-office you describe as
"a pink wedding cake"
and further still, summer stretches
into plantations of banana, coffee fields, cocoons
of cotton. To Patagonia
is an annual journey for the arctic tern, *Sterna Paradisaea*,
stitching the distance between two icy poles,
following the path of the sun.

Probably this tern sees more daylight during its lifetime
than any other animal. It summers in the North while up to
24 hours of daylight daily prevail, and 'winters' in the South
where periods of daylight greatly exceed the hours of darkness.

What I love about this city
is clearest on hot days and in the market:
tubs of truculent lobster, sleeping rabbits,
clatter of coin, sweet pulp of peach against teeth.
Everyone talking and eating, eating and talking,
a pre-European language little more complex
than the persistent wail of babies in prams
or the stutter of pneumatic drills.

They keep digging up the streets here,
have you noticed? "Digging to China",
we used to say. In England,
kids with shovels expect to end up in Australia —
the illusion of Empire, or geographical fact?
I once meant to get an atlas and check it out,
as I did when I first learned that China
was not south.
Down meant *South* to me then;
Down South. Where it is always summer.

* Note: The remarks on the arctic tern are from W. Earl Godfrey, *The*
Birds of Canada (Ottawa: The National Museums of Canada, 1979), p. 191.

ERIN MOURÉ

ANGELUS DOMINI

To say *prophecy*, to say *reason*
& fight out
the length between them,
a broken board for a measure, for an audience
a girl in the fast-food apron, reading a comic on the lawn.
The stale houses of memory shut their doors,
sweepings on the doorstep.
You're swept away by the tide of cars
passing red lights into infinity.
The radio brings back
rock & roll of the sixties,
you turn it up,
curious,
wondering where you stand in this.
It is what you remember.
It is all.
It is all a noise.
It is all over.
The young are
younger than you.
The sum total of reason has not changed
one bit.
& the sum of prophecy:
the time you've wasted, an Incarnation
you couldn't quite manage, divided
by the pell-mell cars

JET

Shapes the mind makes.
Air & houses.
How the house stops & the air
starts,
the body thrown with a lurch,
no transition
no ease
no easiness.

To be in the air, flying,
is to love the man you know
without pursuit.
You make his body turn to you like film,
go forward, break, or stutter
backward into his red car.
Still he does not see you,
his hair uncut, the jacket & old sweater, ripple
His legs under the blue trousers
lift & tauten
The same light presses him again & again
shearing down from the alley.

Shapes of possible, dreams.
You want your dreams real as airports,
cold as rain.
Wherever you are, in dreams or flight
you fear to touch him,
not wanting to ignite
Or frighten him with the shape your mind makes
where your body stops its hurtling
& the air begins,
as your plane lands in his city, its jets reversing
& he does not know you,
keeps walking in the traffic,
does not know

NURTURE

I walk into my life & it is
a stutter without fragments,
short of sleep,
one side of its head dull.
It is the day after migraine.
My body has come back to its life without squalor
just the damp particulars
no one wants,
to squeeze out a few more years.
Outside its rooms on the boulevard
a woman in wide skirts beckons,
pulling lemons out of the willow.
It is the day after
pressing the left skull against a mattress,
holding it still,
not blinking or seeing, void finally of desire

as I wanted, to be
without desire.
To be in a body without feeling,
sick & absent from friends.
I want them to nurture; my body disobeys.
I gain weight when other women's children
swell with worms & cannot defend
against hunger.
In the migraine I hear them ticking;
in the migraine my pain
replaces no one's.
It is more of the same thing, an excess, it is addition
or paint by numbers;
more & more clutter in a bare room,
& I touch my head,
the woman is still outside, she has picked
many lemons from inside the willow,
I don't deserve her,
when she turns to me her skirt is full

STATE OF RESCUE

The sky dark & she is under it,
behind the house
lifting her baby on his birthday, into the home
of her arms;
her body wide in its winter clothing,
her car open & yellow lit
In the house the father roars, cutting up the furniture,
shaking the white crib with his beard;
his wild arms
drunk on whisky, shut up like a jar

The woman is holding the baby into the cold air
beside two policemen at 4am,
putting his diapers into the car,
warming its engine,
scraping ice from the windshield
As the woman moves out, she rescues
herself from fear, rescues
the child whose eyes are caught
in the coat of terror, of furniture breaking in the night
waking the neighbours
to the voice of his father
who is not in heaven, whose name is not clear
whose will is his child
one year old
too frightened to cry till the policeman held him
safe in his mother's car, its engine
a soft sigh in the neighbourhood,
the car's warmth
a red thermal line on the city's scanners,
driven
to a sister's house, & sleep   now
whatever the sky brings, wherever the father is,
whoever he wants to be

HOW I WILL LOOK AT YOU

If light has a certain texture, if you can
weave it in & out of our warm skins
& pull us together,
two figures drowning in a building, the colour,
what it would be
how they would find us
Today Princess Grace of Monaco died,
brain hemorrhage after a car accident.
& the lost family was found in unmarked territory,
burned up, six bones inside their car.
Light, handfuls of light
woven together, the fabric of identity,
I with you,
identify me, touch me, stubborn, my hands

Last night I dreamed I kissed you finally,
unasked for, my desire clumsy,
your skin worn & startling
I held you with my hands to kiss you
& you answered, then pushed me away

So I woke, it was 5am,
your kiss had lifted the light out of my room
out of the sky
into my body, charged with the taut thread
I stole from you, happily
I got up then, dressed & worked alone
the light burned
between my lips
& melted, & turned to daylight, the way
I will look at you this morning,
if I see you, how will they find us,
if you let me be

AMORE

The bats rage up & down the fire escape,
knitting new husbands
shadows without doors
white slats thru which the night leaks
Bless us & these thy gifts, my arms ache,
heavy with the weight
of being flesh, & desiring

The bats are my own wish, unhinged,
hitting dark wings against
the railing
their tiny lungs pumping up & down

Or are they my arms, wanting
to go somewhere
afraid to leave me alone,
who will I touch when my time comes?

It's the bats terrify me.
No more radar, no more adrenalin, no more
chance to run up
the fire escape into the building
kissing the cold doorway
My husband who is not my husband
Holding our divorce up
like a key

SAFETY

Far off in the washroom, the light comes thru, the sound
of him throwing up dinner,
his sickness,
his body so hard it won't digest,
won't welcome food
In the newspaper, a picture of Gilles Villeneuve
in the last second of his life,
his car already demolished,
his body in the air
turned-over
about to slam its bones into the wall
So many kilometres per hour,
with or without the Ferrari.
& the small man in the washroom, who admires
but will not listen
to the fast man who says death is boring.
I can't drive slower, he says.
I drive at my limits, for
the pleasure, purely

& you, in this house, listening to the small man's body
turn over its cylinders,
refusing its food
What part you play here, the pattern,
the man sick with alcohol,
who wants boredom,
who wants to be a dead man in your arms'
bent safety without cure
or derision
the way Villeneuve held his body in the air,
so fast only the camera stopped him

WATCHING NEWSREELS AT THE FARM OR BEIRUT FROM WESTEROSE

The pig eating out of the trough of a
man's head
A pig eating his master
A journalist drinking coffee, mortar
fallen at her door, she keeps
writing
The city is calm tonight
A salesman sells films, the injured smoke
their cigarettes
A tree rises toward the hill
Guns & belts
of cartridge-
shells
Seashells
Powder, metal casings, noun, noun,
death
In the sky, red with the smoke of buildings
afire in the north
Verb, verb   says the sky
Step out of the farmhouse to smell it, forest fire at Loon Lake
Too far for meaning
Why keep
writing
You're safe here

LIGHT-YEARS

So many evenings my signals burn & watch
as the lights flash high in the sky's corridor
in   out of sadness, metal
soaring out of cloud
& I dream
my brother into one of those planes, descending to Vancouver
I dream the tilted ocean, Bowen Island, fishboats
tiny freighters, jewels —
a whole view for him as the plane banks to land
into the green-washed city

Now he's come & gone
The walls & houses have come back to where they were
& shut up their crazy mouths of wonder
A wind has pulled the coat out of the sky
Real stars glint their ancient light
continual

In these hours I have done nothing
Planes inside the night
repeat their being above the ocean, breaking free of storm
In their roar I am quiet & in the company
of childhood gods
left with the spaces my brother filled
where his voice occurs to me, returns & enters
The room smells like coffee
A dream we grew with, to know each other, to meet & talk
without rhetoric;
as actors moving into green, light-years apart,
our gear open for landing,
testing the thin balance our lives are

DOE-FACE

Soft fur of her doe-face in the snow below the rails
Brown on brown body, warm-blooded, still
The cow elk hears the ticking of
her hunger
The animals of prey do not attack her
Know she will die here & they will eat from her
Easy meat
Hit by the passenger train, skidded down
the snowslope into silence
Wild she gazes, soft ears spread out, supplicant among trees
her body alert as the trains speed above
Their track so civilized & named
A siding called Palliser, below it
the elk waits, grass torn from beneath the snow
as far as she could nuzzle,
unable to stand
Already she does not know what her life was, she
becomes the snow, lain in trees under the mountain

It's our emotion, not hers
She doesn't feel the heart welling up
or know she waits to die
That's just us, projecting our own incapacity,
her body still alive
suffering pain without cry or madness
She looks up, her long ears & animal intensity,
legs folded under her,
a brown patch in the white sentence
She watches our train pass,
without coming down from our dangerous track
to know & rescue her from hunger
To touch her
Bringing in our arms, like game wardens,
a warm shot for her

SENTENCES

for Mary Grendys Mouré

1

The short & bumpy sentences of the heart.
Arms of a sweater, bumping
other sweaters in the dark closet.
The crack of air let inside by the dog.
Breathe easy, your mothers
have gone away in cars, dressed in furs, to the sore
hospital of the body.
The heart crouches under the ribs, its beat like a rosary.
You friends have caved in,
their lips are salty, hard; it's hard when
they raise their tongues to you

Speak up!
Your brothers are shaking their father out of the wet
laundry, unfurling him from bed-sheets in the yard,
divorcing him.
He's your father too!

2

The arms of the sweater are   my arms, waiting
patient for the sideways embrace.
The dog left the door open, I can breathe now.
My mother came back & took off her coat,
& hugged me,
knowing how alone I was   & how I cried
when she went away,
to be emptied by hysterectomy

Hey Mary!
Thanks to you I can kiss the salty
lips of my friends, loving them, stuffing my
sweater into them with its wild arms,
guffawing, rejoining
the bumpy heart-tick, my rosary.
My father writes me his long letters freely now,
we talk together about our own name, Mouré.
Even my brothers stumble up into the doorway, a whole
family yapping & not listening,
as if it mattered, Mother —
Let me tell you I am twins with them, holding our arms &
our years up like sentences, coming alive
however apart our births were!

CARDIAC GRIZZLIES

At Banff this summer, the river lunged steeply at us,
ungainly beings picking our bodies across the rocks,
balanced incredibly on the cliff above.
Or alone
the three of us hulked over coffee in the Praha
working our way thru the mood
of each other, the speeches.

Sooner or later the rain falls out of its cupboards
& cries.
Ratty wet sparrows in their summer clothes
pick the earth up in their beaks;
when they shake it out
their heads tremble wildly among the cars.
We sit on the furniture in the rented rooms, three
cardiac grizzlies with our huge heads,
the hair painstakingly combed,
the human   well-learned, tho
our talk sounds like leaves that talk
to leaves, on the dark side of the tree.

Our own wildness by the river, outpouring our own banks too,
the feeling of this tangled getting-together
twice a year, not enough
by a long shot but
better than staying alone, in the rough den of our cardiac lives
on two sides of the Rockies.
It's us,   the crazy silent pawing ones, the ones
that crash thru underbrush to keep myths alive,   capable of
finding each other when we need to,
in uncertain territory
Capable of sustenance & love

FIREHALL #3: HEART ON TRIAL

Today I stand at my window & watch
the firemen pick up hoses with their young arms
Blue-shirted,
mustachioed, in love with the ordinary
tedium, a precision-ballet of work & ladders,
their practice of rescue,
the red brick housing them.

I miss you more than ever.
My heart too
is the red brick, its fertile cells moving in & out,
re-stringing the veins,
counting them, laying the arteries in neat rows,
uniformed, young & sexual
tho the job is ordinary, & the same.

With them I wait to break   out of the red brick
to the fire,
the sirens blazing
Flame dancing again   outside my body,

where you are.   Or
one like you.
Your replacement.
My fire.

TRICKS
for Trix, a dog

This is a life in which
a case of whisky is one drink.
In it, a dog goes totally blind & no one knows
if it remembers its young doghood,
the smell of wild mountains carried in storm
from the high passes

I feel I am in the world & there is no god in it with me.
These days my husband gets up & sits
on the edge of our bed & says
a case of whisky is one drink.
He says there are glasses as big as women filled with rye & he wants
to marry one.
This is what I listen to, no wonder
I can't sleep.
Faintly
I hear the heart-tick of my old dog in Calgary, 800 miles away.
She sleeps on the porch, & shies away when the footsteps
come, crying gently.
When there are no footfalls, she rests & waits to die.

I want to leave my husband & let him marry
all the bottles in Vancouver,
while I go to Calgary to sit beside the blind dog of the family,
her eyes muddy with cataract,
& tell her of her old/young doghood, of hikes to the ice-caves
with a black pup in '71, who was herself
splay-legged on the fireroad.
I want to tell her she is a dog who loved the mountains,
& she should be proud even in blindness
that she saw them & climbed their hard trails,
& camped there with the humans
like a god.
Now she is only afraid, of being stepped on.
She knows our voices, even mine that she hears so seldom.
She speaks back in her small voice
& snuffles nearer.
I wish she would remember & be proud, but she lives
only the present in her dogged blind way,
fighting the back stairs.

Without her memories I am alone in the world, the god gone out of it.
My husband murmurs over, *the root is still there,*
in the whole world there is only whisky for one drink.
No wonder I can't sleep.
No wonder to look at the world is to go blind in it

LIBBY SCHEIER

DWARFS AND WAR

My mood today was to write about dwarfs,
something small, misshapen and very far
from my personal experience. I thought
I'd list details about their large heads,
short trunks, bowed stumpy legs,
then surmise about dwarfs making love
(though I could think of nothing special
that might occur when dwarfs make love).

Instead the September rain got on my nerves,
my muscles ached and all I could think about
was trench warfare, days of rain in gutters
of the Great War, mud in the mouth and the
body trying to fold in on itself,
hovering over the warmth of its own
internal organs and circulation of blood.

Who do you suppose was the great genius
designer of trench warfare? Just imagine
the diagrams and drawings littering his desk
and the dry afternoon discussions
with the other men, no dwarfs in sight.

After the war he left the military
for a career in highway design.
He became very bored with this
and offered his services in the maneuvers
in middle Europe before the Second War.

The Second War was less personal.
It's hard to think of just one body
soaking in the mud. What comes to mind
are skies become smoke and cloud
shading from the sun a million bodies
transformed into jigsaw chunks,
many eyes become white stones.

Why it's easier for me today to write
about war than dwarfs I don't know.
What do I know of war?

Once a small man with a knife raped me,
took my money and tried to kill me.
I felt real fear for the first time.
It comes back sometimes, unexpectedly.

The man who raped me cut my hand.
Later I licked it and tasted blood.
I always liked the taste of my own blood.
But I have no sense of my body

wetting through with rain and dirt
or blood, or my body flying apart while
the eyes watch in the last living seconds.

This muscle-ache of rain
made me think of war.
What made me think of dwarfs
was a poem I just read about dwarfs
and remembering the smallness
of the man with the knife.

CURING CANCER
based on a newspaper account
of Jim Jones' People's Temple

it is now known that you can cure cancer with chicken livers.
you leave some chicken livers in a warm place for three weeks
until they are green and white with rot. then you take the
chicken livers and someone who has cancer and lead them to a
bathroom. you stand by them while they shit or you stick your
hand down their throat to make them puke. then you show the
person the green and white and stinking livers and tell them
they have crapped out their cancer or puked up their cancer.
then the person is cured of cancer. if the person is not cured,
the person is happier dying than they would have been if you
had not shown them the rotting livers. keep that in mind
because in future you will find it useful to explain other things.

PREPARING

eyes in a morning glass,
a foot washed clean of pebbles and sand,
hips encircled with black pearls,
these requirements of freedom I can fulfill:
to sing slightly out of a crystalline
throat, steel-hard and ice-blue,
to balance a gold watch lightly on my head,
to number the days of this month in blue ink,
    next month in black blood, and
    all others in morning light

here is the emerald that touches the
nape of my neck with a lion's touch
here are the phantoms
and pieces of black earth
that graze my hips
inside my elbow a mouth speaks
of feathers and insects

my eyebrows are ready to be singed
my eyes long for the sun

SOME DAYS

I

perhaps I should tell you some things
sometimes your penis loves me
makes me wild, but sometimes
your penis is a bore, a funny blobby thing
I wouldn't want to look at
after too many drinks,
like sausage and eggs on a hangover,
no it won't do, so keep your penis in perspective

some days the violence of sex
cleans me right out

some days I shun you
the days when you come like a giant bear,
hungry and tired, to flatten and feed on me

II

I have my some days too
sometimes your breasts are magic
with their shapes and changes,
the words are warm on your lips
and I listen carefully

some days your words slam at me like doors
you look ugly
your belly still big from the birth
an old jellyfish with one eye
your body a cold lump on the sand

REVERSALS

this love begins to shroud me
your body over mine
is a large mushroom
I am dark and damp and cold
the freedom you once brought me
feels now like
closing walls
the warmth your body gave me
clings and suffocates me now
it is hard to know why
this has happened
why these truths of some years
have turned upside down
but the French kings
were guillotined, the Czar
was murdered, and
capitalism is halfway down
the other side of the mountain
a small thing
like our true love
can also ripen and die

I LIKE

I

I like
your small breasts
they do not frighten me.
your hips are small,
too, tonight
there is not enough
of anything, and my choice
is to be nothing.
then, I want your small
breasts and hips to
touch mine
I want
you
to stand in front of me
perfectly
your nipples at the exact
height as mine
your hip bones in perfect opposition.
then slowly
press against me
flatten my small breasts
with yours, fit
your slim hips between
my wider ones
pass through me to the other side
take the nothing with you

II

Treat me as sky-thin air
falling with dry leaves
let me lie here
a quiet nothing, till
morning speaks of hand-
encircled shapes
let my bulk speak
for itself against
the thin clouds

I have tried to point
my eyes toward the large
carnivorous birds
I have tried to lay hands
on plant roots and the
eggs of insects

III

I see the endpoints
of your body's form, I
see its repetition
of my imperfections
you are my
deadend, mirror-girl, you
sing me one-note songs
of little-girl dreams
you draw me near
the circle's stillborn
center

IV

I see your leaves, dropped
early to the ground, and
hold in my hand your stem,
and break it
I see that you
have fallen early,
and I have gained
a season

A POEM ABOUT RAPE

It's hard to write a poem about rape.
Surprisingly,
having been raped doesn't make it easier.

You can read many outraged tracts about rape,
by women who have been raped,
by anti-rape activists,
by dry theorists of psychology or medicine.

What would be the purpose
if I wrote a poem about rape?
I told my friends and lovers
how I felt after it happened.
These expressions of emotion
were scarcely art.
They were mainly noisy and honest.
They were frustrated because
who knew where the rapist had gone
and only a personal act of violence
would have been balm to my emotions.

I don't feel that I can tell you
anything about rape in a poem about rape.
I can't think of a well-crafted image
that runs from the poem's first line
to its strong but subtly suggestive ending.
I can't think of a list of clever symbols
that would throw a new light on rape
so that you might grasp it, finally.

In fact, it is now so many years
(seven, I think it's seven)
since I was raped that my anger
has waned and cannot feed a poem.
On the other hand, I could not
write about rape until recently.
My brains no longer knock against
my skull when I think about it.
I even said to a demonstrator yesterday
(she was shouting: Castrate rapists!)
well, I don't really agree with that
as a general political slogan, although
when I was raped I wanted to personally
murder the guy and castrate him too.
The order of events was unimportant.
I still feel that would have been
an act of justice.

How can I explain rape to someone

who does not find a midnight streetcar ride alone
frightening, only boring
who does not worry about who gets on
the streetcar, who looks at you,
who gets off when you do.

It's hard to write a poem about rape.
I don't want to write a political tract.
I want you to grasp the experience.
I don't think a poem can do that.
Certainly this poem is not doing it.
This poem is definitely a failure
in bringing the experience of rape
into your living room.

A dramatic re-enactment is not the answer.
A film about rape is not the answer.
These usually excite you anyway
which is not my purpose.
Raping you is not the answer.
There doesn't seem to be any answer.
There doesn't seem to be any answer
I can hand over to you right now.

LIMITS OF THE WEREWOLF

at the full moon, at midnight
her face gives out its secret
beard, her teeth
grow long as the moon rises
and her hands
clench and flex their
hairy joints
she slides slowly
outdoors
her skin open to the air
her night-animal
senses awake as they never were
in her human guise
she is drawn by a fleshy
smell, edges down a street
sees a solitary figure
a man walking
she closes in on him slowly,
crouches
leaps
he turns
eyes two full moons of fear
his body gives out the stink
of fear, she is knocked
back by the stench, falls,
watches her prey run
into shadows
she slinks home, sick
with the smell of fear
the moon fades in the morning
sky, the month has its second
day, she wakes smooth-faced
and calm to her lover's kiss
on her cheek, his
beard brushing
her face softly

THE HARD WORK OF FLYING

I

sit with your legs apart,
he says, and open
your shirt to the fourth button

he arranges her like a still life
some evenings when sex diffuses
in the humid August air

she follows each direction, curious
to see what image will emerge
what objects he will need

to complete the picture
or maybe he will find all the
raw materials right there

on her body or even his.

II

what did you dream last night? he asks.
that I made love to you all night, she says,

very quiet love with a little violence.
he did not dream at all last night
but promises to dream of her tonight

I often dream of flying, she says.
what is your flying like? he asks,
do you glide up like a cloud

while people and objects slowly diminish?
it's not a question of gliding, she says,
I have to work to fly.

my arms beat against the air
like the wings of an infant bird
finally and with difficulty my body lifts

slowly higher and higher above trees
and everything then becomes small
and hazy beneath me

I never dream of flying, he says,
but sometimes my body falls on all fours
and I run at great speed along the streets.

CAROLYN SMART

BLOOD IS SAP IS DESIRE

Blood is sap.
The only kind I know on sight
is mine. I always thought
the Queen would bleed in blue.
My arms look like royal forests,
fine blue trees
that can't hold off the future
from my wrists
anymore than a maple
can hold its sap all year long,
way up in the branches,
spiney fingers
sucking out the sunlight.

Sap is desire.
My body feels empty of you
because I love the curve of your wrist.
I know the pause
longer than a breath and then some
as you wait at the edge
and then like a diver come deep into me
knocking out sounds I don't know
from my searching throat.
I want to come inside you
with more than emotion,
to have your body surround mine,
to have you depend on my deep movements
for your language, your need.
I want to fill you up
from root to blossom,
fill your head with warmth and confusion.
Watch me now,
as I begin to part the leaves
from about your body.

NOW
for Gillian

What you did was take your life and burn.
You, with those dark eyes,
half amused, half afraid.
What becomes of women
who want as much as we?
What are the words for this:
a man comes into your life
and you beat against the darkness in him,
knowing you need it,
you love to see your breath in the dark.
You write until your hand cramps,
another kind of desire.
And you're always questioning the words,
yes, words and the body are traitors.
You slam against another darkness,
oh but the lives of women,
how you love to be with them,
their wild hands and eyes,
the way they make you feel.
You'll never lose yourself in small ways,
no one you love ever does.
But courage, now, as you take
your life to the edge of emotion,
burning with experience of the earth.

OUTSIDE GRAND FORKS, NORTH DAKOTA

We smoke cigarettes and the time passes slowly.
As I am driving, you are doing the talking
and in between, we listen to the radio.
Franco is dead the radio says
and outside, it is thirty below zero,
and the beaten wheat is lying in the fields.
There are no trees here. The road is long and straight
and the cigarettes seem to last forever.

We are lonely for each other
as we drive along, we are lonely
for even ourselves.
We reach the building we are aiming for,
a low white building lying in the shade
of the cold afternoon.
We sit in the crowded waiting room,
the smell of dust on the magazines, the plastic plants.
From time to time the nurse passes by,
an opaque jar in her hands.
Somewhere a girl is screaming,
but no one in the room is listening,
and I cannot talk to you
because it is you who will be screaming
and I'm just here to listen.

You've gone in — I cannot bear to remember
the look we give each other
before you turn the short corner and are gone.

It doesn't take long,
and suddenly I see what it is
that the nurse is carrying,
and she passes me by with this thing in her hands
and she flushes it down the toilet.
I can hear them saying *bring me a bowl,*
she's going to be sick
but you weren't — you were always too proud.
There's your pale face coming towards me,
my arms around your fine body.

Oh my sweet friend
we are lonely for even our childhoods
as we drive towards Canada,
the wind chilling right to our bones.

BLEECKER STREET, NEW YORK CITY

A small tree, the bark crumbling like ash
in the dark air of the city.
Every time you see a tree like that
you think of the cities of your childhood,
the constant travelling.

One day, you think, your real life will begin
because you recognise the place by its trees
and the welcome they have for you.
In the meantime, you visit other people's cities,
you watch them walking in the streets,
you stand outside their restaurants
and feel them applauding them at table.

You find a bar and you sit down
on a wooden bench smelling the restlessness
you've carried in with you.
You try to relieve it with a cool drink
and the cheering words you send
to people you met elsewhere:
do you know this view of the park?
could you live in this skyline?
but what you need
is to be back out on the streets,
under the dusty trees,
looking for something, wanting it.

THE KIND OF MAN YOU ARE

You're the kind of man
who likes to see a woman touch herself.
It pleases you.
I reach out for your skin,
that soft spot under the beard
that smells of summer.
I woke up in the early morning,
the air still filled with lilacs,
and heard her playing the flute.
What did you do then?
She's only 15.
My mind beating against my mind
I want you to tell me about touching.
You teach me how to lay a fire,
it burns all evening long.
I'm sitting there drinking,
watching you learn me.
Every day I'm approaching the dark place,
measuring the distance between us:
you get into your car in the morning
and never look back.
I cross the snowy field to my work,
the cold desk, colder fingers on the keys:
the country I carry in the wall of my head.

AFTERWARDS

My lover in his blond jacket
slips his wide, dry fingers into my clothes.
So: this is what it feels like.
My heart is dry as an onion skin.
I turn my back to him in the morning
knowing already the path
his quiet fingers will make on my skin,
the cutting of the onion, the sheen on the knife.
If words could be as quiet as fingers!
So: it happens this way. Just when I think
I'll answer only to the words of the body,
the questioning of fingers,
I grow lonely for comfort, for phrases.
Turning to him, afterwards, I say I love him.
Anyway, I say it. I say the words
with my eyes on his soft, blond clothes.

"IT WAS SO COLD,
I ALMOST GOT MARRIED."

Graffiti

I

He was so cold.
I couldn't help myself,
I fell in love.
At least this time I knew
it wouldn't last forever.
I said as much to myself
over and over,
as if I was warding off
an evil spirit.

II

It was February.
I live in a cold climate.
Because his body is warmer than mine
I clung to him night after night.
Before he fell asleep,
he'd turn his back to me.
He loved to sleep with the window open.
I'd lie there for hours,
feeling the heat of his back
radiating against me.
Just when I thought
I'd be better off alone,
he'd wake and hold me.
I couldn't help myself.

III

It is such a cold world.
I met a man at a party
who talked of loneliness
and I knew he was lying:
he was just like me.
When he said he loved me,
over and over, night after night,
I almost married him.

GRACE

Grace was the woman paid to love me.
A small soft woman in grey and white
who died with one arm in her sensible coat
in 1963.
She had a close relationship with God
who loved her dearly, as I never did.
Stealing her heart with selfishness,
I gulped her life with my budding mouth.
You don't know how I suffer she'd say
as I'd laugh at her and pull away,
her skin so delicate
my breath would leave a scar.
She was a kind of refugee for love,
distanced by her sexlessness
from any family of her own,
I was her loved one, her darling,
the small baby placed in her happy arms
a week after my birth
and held there one way or another
until 1963
when a train took me away
to a school on the coast
and a life of my own, a history.
She died at Christmas,
on her way to the Carol Service.
She was so loved by God
that He took her with Him, they said,
to eat Christmas dinner in His arms.
But she always loved *me* best, I said.
Grace was the woman paid to love me.

STONING THE MOON   (I)

Rooted to the ground
we never speak of loneliness
we say instead   *darkness*

You are thinking about women you thought
you'd comforted   *Tell me everything* you said
and some do   watching you
in the gardens of their lives
smooth face and thoughtful mind
able now to see little but destruction
tired wife and women who denied you honesty
now you say to me *I thought I knew them*
how can they be capable of this darkness
telling me a fiction of a man
who stoned the moon
Don't lie to me you say
and I love you with a violence

We are blind from a lifetime
of looking at the stars
I have learned nothing
because again I reach for you   the other
Let me tell you the story again
I can live your life but change the names

Last night I felt such comfort
know him for 13 years
we spoke of needs and fear
how hard it is to go on
we said *love* and felt at last unselfish
we lay for hours   gentle
I felt soft for him
thought *this time   yes*
out of my sleep I heard him
what will the neighbours say
then I was on the street
three in the morning thinking
who is this man   a face clothed in darkness
what does he know of choice
when he speaks from his life of violence

Where does the anger go
I will not stone the moon
or use a gun on the man who moans
pussy pussy in the marketplace
I do not beat my head on walls
slash forgive or howl

carry a paper life
talk to the floor with rage
for I can touch the darkness
here with you now
and be afraid

Summer night in this clean city
holds an ordinary woman's life
at her throat   her body taken
by a man without lust
who needs to destroy
what he cannot have   her silence
glossy city any hour filled with fear
no alternative when all they know is hate
the woman's nails in her own palm
taste of blood and shame   she raises her fist
answers a history without gentleness
with only violence

Do not lie to me
then how to word the truth to you
sadness of childhood a weapon and shield
we use on each other
sure of little else
we could laugh or cry

Why are we locked inside these skins
forever   this is   darkness
is the anger of being alive alone
forming a shell of intellect
dressing our bodies with tricks
we try again to say to ourselves
One day eyes will not look outwards
ears in each other's brain
we will eat stars
be blind to risk
your hand will reach me
it will be open

TANGO

I begin with the words
I mold into a life
placing you inside the fantasy
I make love to you constantly
through all the stories of your life
taking only the words you use
a couple of visual images
I've conjured out of what I call
passion

Then I allow myself the deep pleasure
memory   your lips at my ear
you talked of death and prayer
and brought forth both from my skin
you were sugar on my tongue
the fragrance of white lilies
they fill up the room you said
we moved together so slowly
we want everything you said
I was watching your eyes
we want

A childhood memory of evening
colours luminescent
the sound of anything
but what words bring out of the skull
the clarity of innocence
what trust meant before we thought it through
standing in a grove of trees at eighteen
saying to myself *die now   now*
while everything is complete

Your mouth could do magic
the texture of your body on mine
let the house fall in you said
I wish we could die now   like this
I am thirty   still believe in this
in wanting everything   pray you do

TELLING LIES

Drugged with light, the lack of it
or longing, she stays on later than she thought,
charmed by streets familiar with you,
any building haunted by surprising grace,
nostalgia's dusk, autumn, but it's later than that:
she's just waiting for the sight of you

Who wants to hear this,
her wanting you, being tired of it,
the smell of traffic from other lives,
her so static, therefore lying
about anything, whatever holds back loss:
a memory, the narcotic you have become

Her stiff with denial and silence,
drinking it dull in the shade or breeze,
drunk and alone saying to the dream
Shut up   Come in off these mazy streets
It is only one more world's end   lying:
her believing in measureless, fantastic light

A frivolous heart beating once, twice, erratic,
shocked by dependence on you, this need she has
for the sight of you, sound of your voice,
always her watching, windows with their dusty stare,
the dark outside, no one awake to listen:
she's telling lies, truth's a phantom only visible at night

FLYING
for Mary

All our lives they've said we expect too much
from what bone and the spark of cells
will make of a simple life
Two of us so eager for the future we imagine
we smoke the air for speed
anything to get what we want   perfection
Believe we can change the world
with language   a tool to call down the stars
watch them come   eager puppies   to the page
You and I are reckless
wanting to believe in everything
a planet of kindness

Your hand on my arm at a party
touches beyond our public selves
past false conversation   clink of glass on wood
dry taste of food   stories people tell of their lives
later thinking *Why did I say so much*
who will hurt me
but your hand is saying to me
care imagine believe
touching the way women touch each other
for comfort   for rest
This from your small hand   trust
the world we desire

For your birthday I give you
a gathering of friends   never expecting
the gift you will give
Not knowing you change me forever you say
Once   everybody could fly
bright eyes   arms in the air as you talk
saying this perhaps for the first time
with such ease my eyes fill up
relief of shared vision
You a small child clinging to steep rock
head already part of the sky
holding on so tight because you know
with only one brief gesture you could fly
without even trying   floating
only a step away   not surprised by this
not afraid   your concern only for your mother nearby
who has forgotten all she knew about flight
knows terror   you hold onto the earth
choose this   still believe
Once you say to us *everybody could fly*

Then you sit back   hands still   face glowing
four other voices remember dreams and Peter Pan
I could have said
waiting for the light to change
the steering wheel solid in my hands
I saw trees about to burst open
clouds moving too fast above the city
and then I knew what I'd always known
if I just let go the air would take me
I thought I was at the edge of madness
felt the sky pulling and thought it wanted my soul
knew it would be so easy   but I held on

I could have said
again and again it happens
I feel the speed of the planet
as it rolls through space
such silence
the ground under my feet gives up gravity
clouds begin their whirl
I know this all so well
one more step
and I would be   flying

My deepest secret
fear always in the telling
what if they banished me   put me away
like children with golden eyes
who practice levitation
some kind of science fiction or madness
the terror of misunderstanding
You have taken the loneliness of silence from me
with your need to believe
in what this world could be

Bone and the spark of cells
is all we have ever had
We see so clearly what we want
from a simple life
Language and touch bring us closer
to what we once knew before fear
The belief in tenderness   innocence
Remember   one more step and then
the air

ROSEMARY SULLIVAN

AT THE RUINS OF THE CAPUCHINAS

Ruins always move us
more than the standing structures
It is the poignancy
of one more human thing lost
How beautiful this naked stone
stripped and exposed
domes like mouths open to sky
archways holding up air
cracks snaking their surface
with rumours of final disintegration
At the Convent of the Capuchinas
the nuns' cells are the size of graves
and effegies sit in their nuns' garb
praying behind skulls of death
I stand and listen to the dogs bark in the distance
and smells of cooking rise from the town
Sweet voices echo in the tower of retreat like bells
and the nuns are here
Their laughter rings over the brilliant tiles in the sun
They are in the garden gathering flowers from the zapotes
                              for their altars
in the hallways scurrying to supper over each other's heels
One sits in her cell where doors never close
gazing at the blue volcanoes and longing for home
The town didn't want them
young girls taken from poverty to serve God
on the backs of the poor
Their peace lasted thirty years
till the earthquake brought them down
and the death they had been searching for
came to them, no more welcome
in this disguise than in any other

TEMPLE OF THE DOUBLE-HEADED SERPENT: TIKAL

*Anthropologists conjecture that the
high priest was born on the temple and
never descended*

I was born on this lip of stone
jutting out over the jungle
I've never wanted to go down
As a child I would run to the edge to catch the birds
or follow the lizards with my hand along the ledges
and I wondered what earth was like underfoot
it's so cool and soft in the fingers
Now I sit and watch my world
the trees sway like swarms of settled birds
and the sounds drift up to me of the monkey's frenzy
At dawn I watch the fresh god break through the tired mouth of earth
and I draw him up with my will
I am other now
my back as hard as this stone
my eye on everything that moves

THE SAD STORY OF DONA BEATRIZ DE LA CUEVA

Don Pedro died when a horse fell on him in the town of Nocheztlan
When they asked where the pain was he said: *In my soul*
His grief-stricken widow Dona Beatriz had the palace painted with black clay
and all the furniture blacked for nine days of mourning
The court plotted Dona Beatriz's murder
but she countered by having all the conspirators arrested
On the final day of mourning she appointed herself La Sin Ventura
the first governess in the Americas
The peasants were shocked, then frightened when the rains started
and day by day the water fell in sheets
Lightning lashed the city with all the powers of the heavens
At midnight on the tenth day the earth heaved
Agua coughed and sent his mud rolling into the city
In the black coffin palace the unlucky one
flew to the chapel with her daughter and eleven maidservants
but her forty hour reign was ended
The flood and shifting earth brought the battered palace down
around the ears of Dona Beatriz
that women should know God did not mean the city to be ruled by females

HUNTING FOR TROPICAL PLANTS
IN THE GOLFETTA

Dawn shakes the trees awake
and reddens the river to attention
between ink blue mountains
emitting their darkness like smoke.
We set off in the quiet waters
hats in our hands   listening
to the wind advancing down the lake
buffing the water like a soft skin
for the pelicans to scavenge —
Rio Dulce, sweet waters smelling of watermelons
the Jungle is alive with light:
ramon trees turning like hands as we pass
palmleaves like pinwheels spinning
and the lianas as deadly fer-de-lance
lolling from branches
All day we hunted bromelias
gawdy pink parasites that seemed to hide
till suddenly they lit the jungle like flares
We moored the boat and climbed the trees
ripping bromelias from their branches.
They dropped into our canoe like burning suns
and we were a cargo of flowers
lacing through green waters
the suns breaking about our burning shoulders

LAKE ATITLAN

The flutist sits on a bamboo pier in my mind
knees carefully crossed, back straight
facing the water
and suddenly the image moves with the memory
of his playing
notes ride out across clear water slicing the mists
and scaling the blue volcanoes
until all is a rich blue harmony
of sound held like a glass globe
on a recessed shelf of my mind
from where I take it
and play it like a flutist on a bamboo pier

HOTEL LENINGRAD

Kostya I am sorry
our words could not cross
but only stared blankly
with the eyes of hurt animals
I would have liked to hear your violin
only the woman at the end of the corridor
was listening too
You kissed my hair as if you touched
your mouth on foreign soil
and I was your freedom
that would leave you
in the small hotel room
where five people looked across language
and did you understand
Outside the wind is bitter
along the ice-locked Neva
I was less that I should have been
because I did not understand

WINTER NIGHT

Tonight the beach is locked in a winter mind
The black water lips its edges
effacing safe boundaries
Breakers advance in a white violence
threatening our solitude
You walk ahead
a hot flick of breath in the blackness
proclaiming your insistence on mattering
in all this desolating landscape
I will hold to the human you said
We left footprints thinking the sand would absolve us
but the winter beach is hard and holds
the frozen soles of numberless feet
ours among them

IT HAPPENS

Occasionally
the trees will step out at you
as long as you don't expect it
The trick is to be looking the other way
and then not to be afraid
when the shock comes like a hole in the heart
They are so much older
and wiser than you are
When they open their faces
perhaps it's not even you they are talking to
but the yellow mud or the thin webby rain
and you are included in their ritual wheel
because by some kind accident
you have slipped from the cut path
Stay there if you can
You shall see how tenderly they use you

THE MAN WITH EIGHT FINGERS

Can you not see
the way the light lies on that open door?
I want to be there with the light in my mouth
Do you not know the sound there
how empty it can be?
Look at my hands
When I was young
I would tell them I was an angel
and they always believed me
When I hold up my hands
they are balanced like wings
Watch my eyes
Look carefully through them
I can go to a place
as desolate and indifferent as heaven must be
Whatever you want I am elsewhere
counting eight fingers of space between need
You must go
The bodies are moving like vacant flowers in my mind
and I must be there

THE REACHING

In all those years
I never noticed your hands
They are frail at the end of your body
looming like a noise to distract them
They are afraid of being fatally human
and hide behind pale nails like closed eyelids
You talk of the problems of desire
It pulls the body where it doesn't want to go
You tell your hands to stop you
but they have turned to soft thoughts
and betray you with reachings
At this moment they are reaching to me
They are shame-faced, curled with questions
and suddenly they fall liquid into my hands

THE TONGUE

She held her tongue just so
like a small fish that darts
into sunlight in a pool
or like a pink bird in a wet nest
It always looked like a soft surprise
And she had a way of opening her mouth
so that the shadows crawled up and down along it
A little animal, she could turn it on its side
and it would go to sleep quietly
But I always thought as I watched
it play behind the lip
what is it ferreting?
At night I could imagine it transformed
and trawling the dark air with longing

BRONWEN WALLACE

MY SON IS LEARNING TO INVENT

My son is learning to invent
himself   Today he tells me of a time
I took him to hospital and left him
alone there.   He describes how he shook the steel
bars of his crib and cried as I left the room
without looking back.

(He was three.   He had pneumonia
and I was alone.   For a week,
I slept in a chair by his bed.
I only left once to buy him a book
when he was asleep.
The child in the next bed
had tubes in her throat and no one
came to visit her at all.)

My son holds up his hands.   If he could,
he would show me the desperate
welts the crib bars left and the black
square of my back cutting the light
from his eyes.

But I shake my head.

Stalemate.

Sometimes I show him pictures of myself
when I was his age.   There is one
where I sit with my kid brother
in the middle of my grandfather's garden.
This is the one my son likes best,
but he insists that the boy,
my brother, who is fat and freckled,
is himself.

"Don't be ridiculuous," I tell him,
"that's your Uncle Pete."

He tosses the photograph aside
and refuses to lose himself
in family history.   What good is it
to him?   Like that stupid riddle
about the sound of a tree falling
alone in a forest of trees.
The sun that shines over
these other children's heads
might as well be shining over
an empty pasture for all he cares.

In the top right corner of the photograph
is the cornfield where the children played
hide and go seek.
We are still there, of course,
only now it is my son and I
who stalk each other
through the thin, green
leaves that bristle our bare arms
and whisper as they fold behind us, dry
secrets only they understand.

Whose childhood is this, anyway?

When we play in the park, he rides
in a swing so high above my head
the peak of his cap is a dark arrow
aimed at the heart of the sun.

"Look!" he calls

And he lets go.

Only his body sinks through the abrupt
air toward concrete and the horrible
sound my throat can't make.

When the rest of the park
begins to move again
he is sprawled on his stomach
in the grass beyond the swing.

He gets to his feet
and his face is the colour of milk,
his lips sucked in
like an old man's.

I open my mouth, as he looks
up at me, wiping his palms on his jeans.

"Were you scared?" he asks.

My son is learning.

COMMON MAGIC

Your best friend falls in love
and her brain turns to water.
You can watch her lips move,
making the customary sounds,
but you can see they're merely
words, flimsy as bubbles rising
from some golden sea where she
swims sleek and exotic as a mermaid.

It's always like that.
You stop for lunch in a crowded
restaurant and the waitress floats
toward you.   You can tell she doesn't care
whether you have the baked or french fried
and you wonder if your voice comes
in bubbles too.

It's not just women either.   Or love
for that matter.   The old man
across from you on the bus holds
a young child on his knee; he is singing
to her and his voice is a small boy
turning somersaults in the green
country of his blood.
It's only when the driver calls his stop
that he emerges into this puzzle
of brick and tidy hedges.   Only then
you notice his shaking hands, his need
of the child to guide him home.

All over the city
you move in your own seasons
through the seasons of others: old women, faces
clawed by weather you can't feel
clack dry tongues at passersby
while adolescents seethe
in their glassy atmospheres of anger.

In parks, the children
are alien life-forms, rooted
in the galaxies they've grown through
to get here.   Their games weave
the interface and their laughter
tickles that part of your brain where smells
are hidden and the nuzzling textures of things.

It's a wonder anything gets done
at all: a mechanic flails
at the muffler of your car

through whatever storm he's trapped inside
and the mailman stares at numbers
from the haze of a distant summer.

Yet somehow letters arrive and buses
remember their routes.   Banks balance.
Mangoes ripen on the supermarket shelves.
Everyone manages.   You gulp the thin air
of this planet as if it were the only
one you knew.   Even the earth you're
standing on seems solid enough.
It's always the chance word, unthinking
gesture that unlocks the face before you.
Reveals the intricate countries
deep within the eyes.   The hidden
lives, like sudden miracles,
that breathe there.

THE WOMAN IN THIS POEM

The woman in this poem
lives in the suburbs
with her husband and two children
each day she waits for the mail and
once a week receives
a letter from her lover
who lives in another city
writes of roses   warm patches
of sunlight on his bed
Come to me he pleads
I need you and the woman
reaches for the phone
to dial the airport
she will leave this afternoon
her suitcase packed
with a few light clothes

But as she is dialing
the woman in this poem
remembers the pot roast
and the fact that it is Thursday
she thinks of how her husband's face
will look when he reads her note
his body curling sadly toward
the empty side of the bed

She stops dialing and begins
to chop onions for the pot roast
but behind her back the phone
shapes itself insistently
the number for airline reservations
chants in her head
in an hour her children will be
home from school and after that
her husband will arrive
to kiss the back of her neck
while she thickens the gravy
and she knows that
all through dinner
her mouth will laugh and chatter
while she walks with her lover
on a beach somewhere

She puts the onions in the pot
and turns toward the phone
but even as she reaches
she is thinking of
her daughter's piano lessons

her son's dental appointment

Her arms fall to her side
and as she stands there
in the middle of her spotless kitchen
we can see her growing
old like this
and wish for something   anything
to happen   we could have her go
mad perhaps and lock herself
in the closet   crouch there
for days her dresses withering
around her like cast-off skins
or maybe she could take
to cruising the streets at night
in her husband's car
picking up teenage boys
and fucking them in the back seat
we can even imagine
finding her body
dumped in a ditch somewhere
on the edge of town

The woman in this poem offends us
with her useless phone and the persistent
smell of onions   we regard her as we do
the poorly calculated overdose
who lies in a bed somewhere
not knowing how her life drips
through her drop by measured drop
we want to think of death
as something sudden
stroke or the leap
that carries us over the railing
of the bridge in one determined arc
the pistol aimed precisely
at the right part of the brain
we want to hate this woman

but mostly we hate knowing
that for us too it is
moments like this
our thoughts   stiff fingers
tear at again and again
when we stop in the middle
of an ordinary day and
like the woman in this poem
begin to feel
our own deaths
rising slow within us

CHARLIE'S YARD

Some things have an order
that isn't planned. In Charlie's yard
the woodpile leans toward the necessary
laws of gravity enough to keep it
upright, but its true symmetry comes
more from anger: clean bite of it
and the axe in Charlie's hands,
driving deep into the sullen heart
of a solitary night.   After his wife left,
the only things that Charlie brought
from the farm they'd shared
were bits of machinery, scraps he liked
the shapes and colours of. They rust in the green
of his garden now, plow discs and wagon wheels.
Each one has its place somehow, an authority
tranquil as an old man's, who has worked
all his life with his hands, until even his mind
moves around thoughts with the same
unhurried grace. It's like that wicker chair
abandoned in the centre of the yard.   No one intended
to leave it there, just drifted off toward
whatever plans they'd made while sitting in it.
Now, it's rooted there as surely
as the tree behind it, weathered into place
like the bare grey boards of the toolshed.
Some things have an order
that isn't planned. They seem aimless
as the hours a man spends waiting
for the woman he loves,
a pot of coffee going muddy on the stove.
It's just when he's given up
he turns to find her, framed by the white
wood of his doorway and the blue sky
caught in her hair.

INTO THE MIDST OF IT

You'll take a map, of course, and keep it
open in front of you on the dashboard,
though it won't help.   Oh, it'll give mileages,
boundary lines, names, that sort of thing,
but there are places yet
where names are powerless
and what you are entering
is like the silence words get lost in
after they've been spoken.

It's the same with the highways.
The terse, comforting numbers
and the signs that anyone can read.
They won't be any good to you now.
And it's not that kind of confidence
you're after, anyway.

What you're looking for are the narrower,
unpaved roads that have become
the country they travel over, dreamlike
as the spare farms you catch
in the corner of your eye,
only to lose them
when you turn your head.   The curves
that happen without warning
like a change of heart,
as if, after all these journeys,
the road were still feeling
its way through.

A man comes up on your right — blue shirt
patched from the sky — solid and
unsurprised.   He doesn't turn his head
at your passing and by the time your eyes move
to the rear view mirror, the road has changed.
But it's then you begin to notice
other people: women hanging clothes from grey
porches, a clutter of children on the steps.
Like the man, they do not move
as you go by and you try to imagine
how you must look to them: metallic glimmer
on the bright rim of their sky,
disturbing the dust
that settles behind you, slowly,
through the day's heat,
while in your mind's eye, their faces
form and change with the rippling patterns

sun and cloud make on the fields,
like the figures that swim below your thoughts
in the hour between dream and waking.

It makes you think of the people you love,
how their faces look
when they don't know you're watching them,
so that what you see there
forces you to recognize
how useless your love is, how little
all your hopes, your good intentions
can ever do for them.

Only now, this doesn't hurt any more,
becomes part of your love, in a way,
just as the dry-weather drone of the cicada
belongs to the heat, to the dust that sifts
like ash over the shiny leaves.

And, somehow, this is what you need
from the country you're travelling through,
where the farmlands are spread so meagrely
that the crops have a pinched look
as if they drew their nourishment
from the ancient mountain range
and limestone plains that suffer
a few inches of grey soil.
From the road and the way it moves
without altering the landscape
so that houses and barns appear
to grow from the sides of hills
insistent as the rock and almost as indifferent
making all your questions
about why people came here,
what they liked about it,
why they stayed
as meaningless as questions you might ask
of the trees or the earth itself.

You, who have lived your whole life believing
if you made enough plans
you wouldn't need to be afraid,
driving through a countryside
only the road seems to care about,
to rediscover every time it enters
with that kind of love that's partly tenderness
and partly a sort of confidence
you can't put words around.
Like the look

the people at home will give you
when you get there: nonchalant and almost too deep
for you to see, as they turn back
to whatever held them
before you came.

REMINDER

In a crowded theatre lobby, the perfume
in a strange woman's hair nudges a jealousy
I thought I'd put down years ago.
Unlocks that stubborn convolution of my brain
where it rears and spits.
Even my fingers turn to claws.

Smells like fists.
One whiff of feta cheese and olives
numbs my solar plexus with the blow of a first love,
while fresias are a falling into something deeper,
a loss I haven't even named yet.

I'm told that smell is centred
in our first brain.   Primitive,
lizard part of us still cautiously sniffing
its way through colours and mysteries.
The world as it is before we discover
how to shape it into names,
learn to use language like a hope
for the future.   Something that could save us
if we use it carefully, put enough words
between ourselves and the past.

A man and a woman sit in an all night
restaurant. She's smoking cigarettes,
he's drinking cup after cup
of black coffee, double sugar.
They're in one of those conversations
you don't need words to follow,
though they're using enough of them, their mouths
so rigid with choosing that the lips
have thinned to that whiteness you find
outside pain, if you tighten your muscles hard enough.

And maybe it's only because I can't hear
what they're saying that I imagine
this other sound, somewhere between a feeling
and a voice. An ache in the bone that sings
of an old wound.   Something you can't put
your finger on.   Right now, it's cautionary,
like a growl, though already their bodies
cringe at it and their hands ride
the waves of its swelling.

Sooner or later it will
rise and she'll start screaming;
he'll retreat into that baffled
silence men sometimes use for tears.

This isn't a lesson in body language.
It's more like a warning, though there's not
much we can do.   We can't go back
to nuzzling and grunting at each other,
trying to sniff out anger or love.
And there's no such thing
as a simpler time, anyway.

You might call it
a reminder, like the dinosaur
bone in the museum,
the one we can touch,
the one worn smooth
with our need.

Meanwhile, the man and woman go on
talking and I can imagine how their mouths
must ache for a word that's as explicit
as the click of her lighter,
his definitive way of measuring
the two teaspoonsful of sugar.
Words are their hope for the future.
They've cherished them like children.
And now their faces have the puzzled,
fragile look of parents
who have taken great care
and are always surprised
to see the past they thought
they'd freed their children from
assert itself. In their way of walking,
in their laughter,
in their sullen, indifferent eyes.

LIKE THIS

It's one of those moments we all recognize
sooner or later and always
in the midst of something
so mundane we aren't prepared
to have it open underneath our feet,
become the classic pratfall victims,
Coyote so intent on catching
Roadrunner he doesn't notice
he's walking on air past the edge
of the cliff.   Right now, we can watch
this man: slim, blond, mid-thirties,
sitting alone at the table, drinking a beer,
reading cookbooks.   He's planning a dinner party
— the first one since his separation —
and he wants to use that recipe for
cucumber soup his wife used to make.
It'll be perfect for the meal
he's planned: glazed chicken and rice pilaf.

He can't find it, of course.
It's probably in one of the books she took
or scribbled on a piece of paper, stuck
in the back of a drawer in their old house.

He can also see there's lots of others
worth trying in these books.

He even knows he could call her up
and ask her for the goddamn recipe
if he wanted to.

Which he does.

But won't.

She'd give it to him.
He knows that.
And she wouldn't ask any questions either,
or make any tacky comments.
In fact, she'd probably be really pleased
to think he'd remembered.

And that's just it.
He tries to imagine the conversation, but
the words he'd have to use
and what they might mean
knot in his head
like the fist he feels
in his chest sometimes
when he thinks of her.

When the man hurls his beer bottle
at the kitchen wall,
the explosion of beer and glass
is almost as surprising
as the cry
that splits his throat
at the same time.

We half expected it, of course,
just as we know that now,
a second later, the wet spot on the wall
begins to look foolish and the puddles
of beer and glass are just another mess
he'll have to clear
before his friends come.

We can see that
even as we understand
how good it felt.

As for the cry
and where it comes from,
we think we recognize that too,
but it won't help.   Sooner or later
it'll be our turn.   Face up against
the event in our own lives
that can't be expiated
and we'll forget about this man,
this voice we think we hear so
clearly now, saying
sorry
saying *Look, I've changed.*
saying *Isn't that enough?*

Well?

Isn't it?

ONE MORE LAST POEM FOR THE DEAD

Like the last glass of water,
and the absolutely last
look in the closet for the bear
that keeps my son from sleep each night,
this is my last poem
for the dead.

I want them to settle down,
I want them to sink without crying
into the dreams I have imagined for them.
I want them to let me go.

What more can I do for any
of them?   For the perfect
suicides: the one who chose a site
only a stranger would happen upon,
packed all his clothes and left
an airtight insurance policy
for his kids.   Or the other, who jumped
clear of the wall and the rocks below it
into a death so deep
they never found her body.
What can I make of someone
who makes dying that thoughtful,
as if it were just another means of tidying something
they couldn't fix any other way?

Why do I keep on
going over it and over it, frantically
sometimes, like a new mother
trying to comfort a fussy baby?

The woman who died alone
in her downtown apartment
was tough as death itself.
All her life, she'd fought
anything that needed fighting.
Even in death she managed
with the last pulse of blood
to push her living through
the nerve ends of a continent.
The telephone wires so alive
with the news that when we heard it,
it was her arms that held
us up, and the tenacious vigor
of her laughter that comforted us.

I know death got a fight
for the money that time and yet

in my fears she lies
like someone so badly hurt
that even sleep is a constant fretting
at the tether of her pain.

I write this to convince myself
there's nothing I can do
for her. For any of them.
Even for the one
whose death is a taste in my mouth,
a smell as intimate as a lover's
on my skin.   Even for her who died
with such grace there wasn't room
for praying, and whose loss I carry
under my ribs, fiercely,
like the woman who has lost many children
and carries another, knowing this is her last
chance.   A woman who refuses
even to consider names,
because of the terrible power
words can have.

Even with her, I tell you
I am almost ready
to speak of the future.

This is my last poem for the dead.
I want them to leave me
with the solemn thoroughness
of children, after long summer days,
who fall asleep over dinner,
unable to finish dessert.

I say this is the last.   And yet
I hesitate,
the way sometimes I hesitate
outside my son's room,
after the absolutely final hug,
and listen to him murmur into sleep.
Stand there, part of me longing
for my book and the waiting cup of coffee,
part of me wishing he'd call me
one more last time.

A SIMPLE POEM FOR VIRGINIA WOOLF

This started out as a simple poem
for Virginia Woolf   you know the kind
we women writers write these days
in our own rooms
on our own time
a salute   a gesture of friendship
a psychological debt
paid off
I wanted it simple
and perfectly round
hard as an
egg   I thought
only once I'd said egg
I thought of the smell
of bacon grease and dirty frying pans
and whether there were enough for breakfast
I couldn't help it
I wanted the poem to be carefree and easy
like children playing in the snow
I didn't mean to mention
the price of snowsuits or
how even on the most expensive ones
the zippers always snag
just when you're late for work
and trying to get the children
off to school on time

a straightforward poem
for Virginia Woolf   that's all
I wanted really
not something tangled in
domestic life the way
Jane Austen's novels tangled
with her knitting   her embroidery
whatever it was she hid them under
I didn't mean to go into all that
didn't intend to get confessional
and tell you how
every time I read a good poem
by a woman writer I'm always peeking
behind it trying to see
if she's still married
or has a lover at least
wanting to know what she did
with her kids while she wrote it
or whether she had any

and if she didn't if she'd chosen
not to or if she did did she
choose and why   I didn't mean
to bother with that
and I certainly wasn't going
to tell you about the time
my best friend was sick in intensive care
and I went down to see her
but they wouldn't let me in
because I wasn't her husband
or her father   her mother
I wasn't family
I was just her friend
and the friendship of women
wasn't mentioned
in hospital policy
or how I went out and kicked
a dent in the fender of my car
and sat there crying because
if she died I wouldn't be able
to tell her how much I loved her
(though she didn't and we laugh
about it now) but that's what got me
started I suppose wanting to write
a gesture of friendship
for a woman for a woman writer
for Virginia Woolf
and thinking I could do it
easily   separating the words
from the lives they come from
that's what a good poem should do
after all and I wasn't going to make excuses
for being a woman blaming years of silence
for leaving us
so much to say

This started out as a simple poem
for Virginia Woolf
it wasn't going to mention history
or choices or women's lives
the complexities of women's friendships
or the countless gritty details
of an ordinary woman's life
that never appear in poems at all
yet even as I write these words
those ordinary details intervene
between the poem I meant to write
and this one   where the delicate faces

of my children faces of friends
of woman I have never even seen
glow on the blank pages
and deeper than any silence
press around me
waiting their turn

THE CONTRIBUTORS

ROO BORSON, born in 1952. She is author of four books: *Landfall* (1977), *In the Smoky Light of the Fields* (1980), *Rain* (1980), *A Sad Device* (1981). She won the first prize for poetry in the 1982 CBC Literary Competition.

MARILYN BOWERING was born in Winnipeg, Manitoba and grew up on Vancouver Island. She has published five books of poetry (most recently, *Giving Back Diamonds*, 1982) and one book of fiction. After living and working in a number of different countries, including Greece, Scotland, and the U.S.A., she has returned to live in Sooke, B.C. near Victoria. She is currently working on several fictions and a New and Selected Poems. Her book, *Grandfather Was A Soldier*, is being produced by B.B.C. Radio 3 as a Remembrance Day special.

JAN CONN, born in the Eastern Townships in Quebec, she has lived in Montreal, Vancouver, and is currently in Toronto. Poems of hers have appeared in over a dozen Canadian literary magazines and journals. A first book of poems, *Road of Smoke*, will be published spring, 1984, by Colophon Books, Vancouver. She received a short term writing grant from the Canada Council to cycle through Japan for two months during 1982. A second manuscript, *Red Shoes in the Rain*, recently published, includes several poems from this trip. She is presently working on a Ph.D. in the Botany Department at the University of Toronto. Her research involves black flies that vector a nematode which causes river blindness in Central and South America.

LORNA CROZIER, born in 1948 in Swift Current, Saskatchewan, has published several books as Lorna Uher, including: *Crow's Black Joy*, NeWest Press, 1978, which won the Saskatchewan Department of Culture and Youth poetry prize; *No Longer Two People* (with Patrick Lane), Turnstone Press, 1979; and, *Human and Other Beasts*, Turnstone Press, 1980. Her latest collection, *The Weather*, was published by Coteau Books, 1983.

SUSAN GLICKMAN was born in 1953 and grew up in Montreal. After seven years abroad she took up residency in Toronto, where she has been successively a book editor, graduate student and a professor at the University of Toronto. Her poetry has appeared widely in American and Canadian periodicals, including: *The Canadian Forum*, *This Magazine*, *Descant*, *Quarry*, *Matrix*, *Prism International* and *Event*; and has been anthologized in *Aurora: New Canadian Writing 1980* (Doubleday) and *The Inner Ear* (Quadrant, 1982). Her first book, *Complicity*, is from Signal Editions (1983).

ERIN MOURÉ was born in Calgary in 1955 and presently works for the railroad and lives in Vancouver. She has published three books of poetry: *Empire, York Street* (House of Anansi, 1979), *The Whisky Vigil* (Harbour Publishing, 1982), and most recently *Wanted Alive* (House of Anansi, 1983).

LIBBY SCHEIER is a writer, editor and reviewer whose work has appeared in *Toronto Life, Tamarack Review, Descant, Books in Canada, Prism International, Dalhousie Review* and many other periodicals. She was born and grew up in New York City and lived in California, France, and Israel before settling in Toronto in 1975 where she intends to stay "for the duration". She has a B.A. in philosophy and French from Sarah Lawrence College, an M.A. in English from the State University of New York at Stony Brook, and also studied for a year at the Sorbonne. She has recently published a collection of poems entitled *The Larger Life* (Black Moss Press).

CAROLYN SMART was born in England in 1952. She currently lives in Elginburg, Ontario, writing poems, reviews, and a regular column for *Poetry Canada Review*. She is associate editor of the feminist quarterly *Fireweed*. Her published collections include *Swimmers In Oblivion* (York Publishing, 1981) and *Power Sources* (Fiddlehead Poetry Books, 1982). She is at work on a manuscript of poetry entitled *Stoning The Moon*.

ROSEMARY SULLIVAN, born in Montreal, teaches at University of Toronto, wrote *The Garden Master*, 1975, a study of Roethke; she is an editor with *This Magazine* and *Descant*, co-ordinator of the Writer and Human Rights Conference in Toronto, 1981. She has published widely in periodicals including: *Critical Quarterly, Descant, Montreal Review, Toronto Life*, etc. and in the anthology *To Say the Least*, edited by P.K. Paige.

BRONWEN WALLACE's latest book is *Signs of the Former Tenant*, Oberon, 1983. She is the winner of the National Magazine Award for Poetry, 1980. Bronwen lives in Kingston, Ontario, where she also (occasionally) makes films. Her documentary *All You Have to Do* (co-directed with Chris Whynot) won a Red Ribbon at the American Film Festival 1982.